ONE-DISH
WONDERS

ONE-DISH WONDERS

150 Fresh Takes on the Classic Casserole

By the Editors of Southern Living

©2015 Time Inc. Books
Published by Oxmoor House, an imprint of Time Inc. Books
1271 Avenue of the Americas, New York, NY 10020

Southern Living is a registered trademark of Time Inc. Lifestyle Group.

Writer: Danny S. Bonvissuto
Senior Editor: Katherine Cobbs
Editor: Sarah A. Gleim
Editorial Assistant: April Smitherman
Assistant Project Editor: Melissa Brown
Art Director: Christopher Rhoads
Designer: Anna Christian
Compositors: AnnaMaria Jacob, Anna Moe
Executive Photography Director: Iain Bagwell
Senior Photographer: Hélène Dujardin
Photographer: Victor Protasio
Senior Photo Stylists: Kay E. Clarke, Mindi Shapiro Levine
Photo Stylists: Cindy Barr, Amanda Widis
Food Stylists: Nathan Carrabba, Victoria E. Cox,
    Margaret Monroe Dickey, Stefanie Maloney,
    Catherine Crowell Steele
Test Kitchen Manager: Alyson Moreland Haynes
Assistant Production Director: Sue Chodakiewicz
Senior Production Manager: Greg A. Amason
Copy Editors: Norma Butterworth-McKittrick,
    Adrienne Davis
Proofreader: Polly Linthicum
Indexer: Nanette Cardon
Fellows: Laura Arnold, Nicole Fisher, Loren Lorenzo,
    Olivia Pierce

ISBN-13: 978-0-8487-4544-8
ISBN-10: 0-8487-4544-2
Library of Congress Control Number: 2015946730

Printed in the United States of America
10 9 8 7 6 5 4 3 2 1
First Printing 2015

CONTENTS

INTRODUCTION

Casserole: The word alone is bound to conjure up memories of meals past. Casseroles, after all, are the one category of food that nourishes us in times of both joy and sadness—the birth of a new baby, a church potluck, Thanksgiving dinner, the death of a loved one. They're the comfort food equivalent to Southern hospitality.

The best casseroles are bubbly, gooey, creamy, and cheesy, and are appreciated as much for their convenience as their versatility. You can create a casserole from just about anything—whether you build it using leftovers in the fridge or follow your grandmother's famous lasagna recipe—just toss together a few veggies, a starch, and perhaps a meat, and you have a complete meal. But for those many reasons we love the casserole, the same qualities have also given them a bad rap. Countless recipes call for canned "cream of something" soups and over-processed foods, and casseroles are often seen as heavy and unhealthy. The good news is there is a whole new breed of casseroles, and they're hearty and healthy, simple and sophisticated.

In *One-Dish Wonders*, "casserole" isn't code for getting out the can opener—each recipe is a thoughtful combination of ingredients gathered from the garden and the grocery store. Casseroles can be a bubbly breakfast bake of eggs, vitamin-packed collard greens, and creamy grits dotted with white Cheddar; a rich shrimp risotto full of fresh garlic and thyme; a warm lasagna layered with zucchini, mushrooms, and red and yellow bell peppers; or mini cobblers filled with berries, baked, and served in small skillets.

Just as a great meal brings special people together, a great casserole brings special ingredients together. *One-Dish Wonders* combines the best classic and current culinary trends in a casserole cookbook that shows you how to make them, bake them, serve them, and even swap them.

CASSEROLES 101

Before you shop or chop, take this quick-and-easy casserole "class" where you will learn insider tips, updated recipes, and baking basics.

Tool School

Nothing is more important in the kitchen than the right tools for the right job. All six pieces of equipment below may not be essential to preparing every casserole, but they certainly make whipping up a chicken potpie and all the fixings a lot easier.

BAKING DISHES come in all shapes and sizes, but start with a standard, ovenproof 13- x 9-inch glass or metal pan. Change things up if you want by using individual ramekins, or round, oval, and even brightly colored baking dishes.

A great pair of **KITCHEN SHEARS** can do everything from snip fresh herbs and trim fat from meat to chop canned tomatoes and cut pastry dough. Dishwasher-safe shears are essential for good kitchen sanitation and preventing cross contamination.

MEASURING CUPS AND SPOONS are must-haves for casserole cooking. Need to save shelf and drawer space? Get one clear liquid measuring cup with quantities marked on the side, and a set of nesting measuring spoons.

BOX GRATERS are major multitaskers. They grate cheese and chocolate, and they make zesting citrus a snap. But most also have a large slicing blade and can do the same work as a mandolin—churn out thin slices of veggies, potatoes, and cheese.

Chop your chopping time in half with a **FOOD PROCESSOR**, which makes short work of big batches of vegetables. They're also ideal for grating big blocks of cheese in seconds, and making homemade piecrust and pasta dough, fresh breadcrumbs, and more.

Fresh salad on the side? Yes. Wet salad on the side? No. Use a **SALAD SPINNER** to dry those rinsed greens in a flash. But don't stop there. You can use that same salad spinner to dry out freshly washed herbs, fruits (like berries), and even pasta.

Five ways to Rock that Casserole

It's not an empty baking dish—it's a blank canvas ready to become a delicious work of art. Make it a masterpiece!

1. Gather all the ingredients in one place before assembling your casserole—that includes all food and cookware. Digging in the fridge for this and reaching into the pantry for that adds unnecessary steps that slow down the process.

2. Potatoes, carrots, and other root vegetables often need a little more lovin' in the oven than other produce. Parcook (or partially cook) them ahead before including so they're on the same page with everything else.

3. Fresh or frozen vegetables are often full of extra water that ends up at the bottom of the dish. Thaw and strain frozen vegetables, precook mushrooms and bell peppers, and give those greens a good squeeze.

4. Prefer your pasta al dente? Cut a few minutes off the cooking time so it doesn't overcook when baking.

5. Finish on a fun note: Up the flavor factor by adding crumbled bits of bacon, crushed potato chips, or buttered breadcrumbs on top.

Freezing: The Cold, Hard Truth

Making two casseroles and freezing one? Avoid leaving both dishes in the cold with these genius tips:

- Line the baking dish you plan to freeze with heavy-duty aluminum foil, allowing foil to extend over each side. Lightly grease foil.
- Prepare the casserole as directed, using prepared foil-lined dish. Do not bake. Freeze unbaked casserole until firm.
- Remove the foil-covered frozen casserole from the baking dish; fold foil over top of casserole.
- Wrap in additional foil, or place foil-wrapped casserole in a zip-top plastic freezer bag, seal, and return to freezer.
- When ready to use, remove all foil from frozen casserole, and place in a lightly greased baking dish; cover.
- Thaw in refrigerator for 24 hours; let stand 30 minutes at room temperature, and bake as directed.

Crack the Casserole Code

Casseroles have a language of their own. Get looped in on the lingo.

WHAT: "Cover and chill"
WHERE: The fridge
HOW: Casseroles love to be made ahead of time, which means covering the dish, and chilling it in the fridge. No lid? No problem. Use heavy-duty aluminum foil or plastic wrap to seal the deal.

WHAT: "Overnight"
WHERE: The fridge
HOW: To humans, overnight means sundown to sun up. For casseroles, it means 24 hours.

WHAT: "Take the chill off"
WHERE: The counter
HOW: All casseroles—whether they've been refrigerated overnight or previously frozen—need to rest before hitting the oven. Unless the recipe states otherwise, give them 30 minutes on the counter before baking, and use that time to preheat the oven.

WHAT: "Cover and freeze"
WHERE: The freezer
HOW: Baby, it's cold inside! Use heavy-duty aluminum foil to cover your casserole before sending it into subzero temps.

WHAT: "Start thawing"
WHERE: The fridge
HOW: Ready to break out that casserole you were so smart to freeze? Plan ahead. Unless the recipe states otherwise, let it spend 24 hours in the fridge before baking.

WHAT: "Bake"
WHERE: The oven
HOW: Casseroles bake best without a cover, so remove the lid unless the recipe says otherwise.

Doctor that Dish!

The best dish is the one you create with your family and friends in mind. Use the recipes in One-Dish Wonders as a blueprint, and let your creative juices flow. Recipe calls for Gouda but your kids love Cheddar? Sub it out. Other easy adaptations include swapping canned soup for a prepared Alfredo sauce and using protein-rich almonds as a textured topping.

SIDE PROJECTS

Casseroles may be the stars of the show, but these simple sides shine as the supporting cast.

Fresh Lemon Vinaigrette

Break out that salad spinner and toss those leaves with this light, bright dressing.

WHISK together ¼ cup fresh lemon juice; 1 tsp. Dijon mustard; 1 large garlic clove, pressed; and ¼ tsp. each sugar and freshly ground black pepper. Add ⅓ cup olive oil in a slow, steady stream, whisking constantly until smooth. Store in refrigerator up to 1 week; let stand at room temperature 20 minutes, and whisk just before serving. (Makes about ⅔ cup)

Garlic-Herb French Bread

Warm, crusty bread makes a great scoop for those last bites clinging to the plate!

PREHEAT oven to 350°. Stir together 3 minced garlic cloves, 2 Tbsp. extra virgin olive oil, 2 Tbsp. melted butter, and ½ tsp. dried crushed red pepper. Cut 1 (12-oz.) French bread loaf in half lengthwise. Brush cut sides with garlic mixture; place on a baking sheet. Bake at 350° for 20 to 25 minutes or until golden brown. Sprinkle with chopped fresh chives. (Serves 6 to 8)

Perfect Green Beans

Ready in a snap, these bright green beans add vibrant color and fresh texture when paired with any casserole.

COOK 1 lb. French green beans (also called haricots verts) covered in boiling salted water for 3 to 5 minutes or until crisp-tender; drain and sprinkle with freshly ground black pepper. (Serves 4 to 6)

Easy Sesame Rolls

Nutty sesame seeds give these creative crescents an earthy flavor and enticing look alongside any casserole.

PREHEAT oven to 375°. Unroll crescent roll dough from 2 (8-oz.) cans refrigerated crescent rolls. Separate into 16 triangles, roll up, and place 2 inches apart on a baking sheet. Brush with 2 Tbsp. melted butter, and sprinkle with 2 Tbsp. sesame seeds. Bake at 375° for 12 to 14 minutes or until golden brown. (Makes 16 rolls)

souper stars:
DIY SAUCES

For a fully from-scratch flavor, use these awesome homemade soups and sauces instead of their canned counterparts.

Easy Chicken Stock *(pictured on page 16)*

HANDS-ON: 10 MIN. ✦ **TOTAL:** 1 HR., 30 MIN.

2 lb. chicken wings
2 (32-oz.) containers chicken broth

1. Preheat oven to 400°. Arrange chicken wings on a baking sheet; bake for 20 to 25 minutes or until browned. Bring chicken and chicken broth to a boil in a large saucepan over high heat. Reduce heat to medium-low, and simmer 30 minutes. Pour stock through a wire-mesh strainer; discard wings. Cool stock completely. Use immediately, refrigerate in an airtight container up to 3 days, or freeze up to 3 months. (Makes about 8 cups)

Cream of Chicken Soup *(pictured on page 17)*

HANDS-ON: 36 MIN. ✦ **TOTAL:** 1 HR., 36 MIN.

Use 1 cup of this intensely flavorful homemade cream of chicken soup as a substitute for 1 (10.5-oz.) can of condensed soup in casseroles.

1 Tbsp. canola oil
¾ lb. chicken wings (about 8)
1 small onion, cut into large pieces
1 stalk celery, cut into large pieces
1 clove garlic, crushed

3 cups Easy Chicken Stock
⅓ cup all-purpose flour
1 cup heavy cream
½ tsp. table salt
¼ tsp. freshly ground black pepper

1. Heat oil in a Dutch oven over medium-high heat. Add chicken wings; cook, stirring frequently, 8 minutes or until browned. Stir in onion, celery, and garlic. Cook 5 minutes or until browned. Add chicken stock, stirring to loosen browned bits from bottom of pan. Bring to a boil; reduce heat to medium-low, cover, and simmer 1 hour. Strain stock mixture through a wire-mesh strainer using the back of a spoon to press solids and squeeze out broth. Return stock mixture to pan. Remove meat from bones; add meat to broth. Discard remaining solids.

2. Whisk together flour and heavy cream. Gradually add cream mixture to stock mixture, whisking until blended. Stir in salt and pepper. Bring to a boil; cook 3 minutes or until slightly thickened. Reduce heat to medium-low, and simmer, stirring occasionally, 15 minutes or until thickened. (Makes 2½ cups)

Cream of Mushroom Soup (pictured on page 17)

HANDS-ON: 45 MIN. ✦ **TOTAL:** 1 HR., 5 MIN.

This decadent, creamy mushroom soup gets a boost of flavor from dried mixed mushrooms, fresh cremini mushrooms, and Marsala wine. It's a great alternative to canned condensed cream of mushroom soup. Just substitute 1 cup of homemade soup for every 1 (10.5-oz.) can in the recipe's ingredient list.

3 cups Easy Chicken Stock, divided

2 (0.75-oz.) packages dried mixed mushrooms

¼ cup butter

3 Tbsp. chopped shallots

½ (8-oz.) package sliced cremini mushrooms

2 garlic cloves, minced

¼ cup Marsala or dry white wine

⅓ cup all-purpose flour

1 cup heavy cream

½ tsp. table salt

¼ tsp. freshly ground black pepper

Chopped fresh parsley (optional)

1. Bring 2½ cups chicken stock to a boil in a medium saucepan. Add dried mushrooms; reduce heat to medium, and simmer 5 minutes. Remove from heat; let stand 20 minutes. Remove mushrooms with a slotted spoon; reserve soaked mushrooms for another use. Pour mushroom liquid through cheesecloth-lined wire-mesh strainer; reserve liquid.

2. Melt butter in a Dutch oven over medium heat. Add shallots, and cook 3 minutes or until softened. Add fresh mushrooms; cook, stirring occasionally, 4 minutes or until mushrooms are browned. Stir in garlic; cook 1 minute. Stir in wine; cook 2 minutes or until liquid almost evaporates. Stir in flour; cook 1 minute. Gradually add mushroom liquid and remaining ½ cup chicken stock, whisking until blended. Stir in heavy cream, salt, pepper, and parsley, if desired. Bring to a boil; reduce heat to medium-low, and simmer 20 minutes or until thickened to desired consistency. (Makes 2½ cups)

Basic Marinara

HANDS-ON: 17 MIN. ✦ **TOTAL:** 1 HR., 12 MIN.

3 cups chopped yellow onions
    (about 3 medium)
3 Tbsp. olive oil
1 Tbsp. sugar
3 garlic cloves, minced
5 tsp. freshly ground Italian
    seasoning

2 tsp. table salt
2 Tbsp. balsamic vinegar
2 cups low-sodium fat-free
    vegetable broth
3 (28-oz.) cans no-salt-added
    crushed tomatoes

1. Sauté onions in hot oil in a large Dutch oven over medium-high heat 5 minutes or until tender. Add sugar and next 3 ingredients; sauté 1 minute. Stir in vinegar; cook 30 seconds. Add broth and tomatoes. Bring to a boil; reduce heat to low, and simmer, stirring occasionally, 55 minutes or until sauce thickens. (Makes 11 cups)

NOTE: *We tested with McCormick Italian Herb Seasoning Grinder (set on medium) and Dei Fratelli Crushed Tomatoes.*

Easy Cheese Sauce

HANDS-ON: 25 MIN. ✦ **TOTAL:** 25 MIN.

⅓ cup dry vermouth*
1 garlic clove, minced
3 cups half-and-half
3 Tbsp. cornstarch
1 tsp. kosher salt

½ tsp. freshly ground black
    pepper
2 cups (8 oz.) shredded pepper
    Jack cheese

1. Bring vermouth and garlic to a boil in a large skillet over medium-high heat; reduce heat to medium-low, and simmer 7 to 10 minutes or until vermouth is reduced to 1 Tbsp.

2. Whisk together half-and-half and cornstarch. Whisk half-and-half mixture, salt, and pepper into vermouth mixture; bring to a boil over medium-high heat, whisking constantly. Boil, whisking constantly, 1 minute or until mixture is thickened. Add pepper Jack cheese. Reduce heat to low, and simmer, whisking constantly, 1 minute or until cheese melts and sauce is smooth. Remove from heat, and use immediately.

* Dry sherry may be substituted.

PIE SOCIETY

Flour, butter, salt, and water are all you need to elevate your casserole with a handcrafted crust.

Simple Piecrust

HANDS-ON: 8 MIN. ✦ **TOTAL:** 1 HR., 40 MIN.

1¼ cups all-purpose flour
½ cup cold butter, cut into pieces
¼ tsp. table salt
4 to 5 Tbsp. ice water

1. Combine first 3 ingredients in a bowl with a pastry blender until mixture resembles small peas. Sprinkle ice water, 1 Tbsp. at a time, over surface of mixture in bowl; stir with a fork until dry ingredients are moistened. Shape into a ball; cover and chill 30 minutes.

2. Preheat oven to 425°. Roll dough into a 13-inch circle (or to shape of desired baking dish) on a lightly floured surface. Fit into baking dish; fold edges under, and pinch to crimp.

3. Line pastry with aluminum foil, and fill with pie weights or dried beans. Bake at 425° for 15 minutes. Remove weights and foil; bake 5 to 10 more minutes or until golden brown. Cool completely on a wire rack. (Makes 1 [9-inch] piecrust)

Cheddar Piecrust

HANDS-ON: 10 MIN.   ✦   **TOTAL:** 1 HR., 40 MIN.

1¼ cups all-purpose flour

⅓ cup cold butter, cut into pieces

½ tsp. table salt

¾ cup (3 oz.) shredded white Cheddar cheese

4 to 5 Tbsp. ice water

1. Combine first 3 ingredients in a bowl with a pastry blender until mixture resembles small peas. Stir in cheese. Sprinkle ice water, 1 Tbsp. at a time, over surface of mixture in bowl; stir with a fork until dry ingredients are moistened. Shape into a ball; cover and chill 30 minutes.

2. Preheat oven to 425°. Roll dough into a 13-inch circle (or to shape of desired baking dish) on a lightly floured surface. Fit into baking dish; fold edges under, and pinch to crimp.

3. Line pastry with aluminum foil, and fill with pie weights or dried beans. Bake at 425° for 15 minutes. Remove weights and foil; bake 5 to 10 more minutes or until golden brown. Remove from oven to a wire rack, and cool completely (about 30 minutes). (Makes 1 [9-inch] piecrust)

PIE STYLE

Add some personality to that pie with these decorative topping ideas.

How to make a **perfect lattice crust**

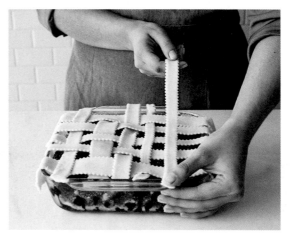

TRADITIONAL: Cut dough into 8 (1-inch-wide) strips. Weave strips in a lattice design over filling, leaving a ½- to 1-inch space between strips. Crimp edge of crust. (*See page 215 for step-by-step instructions on mastering the lattice piecrust.*)

IRREGULAR: Cut dough into 10 to 15 strips of varying sizes. Weave strips in a lattice design over filling, leaving ½-inch to 1-inch space between strips. Crimp edge of crust.

TIGHT: Cut dough into 11 (1-inch-wide) strips. Weave strips in a lattice design over filling, leaving as little space as possible between strips. Crimp edge of crust.

CUTOUT DOUBLE: Using a small cookie cutter, cut out 6 to 10 shapes from dough center. Place dough over filling; fold edges under, and crimp edge of crust. Place cutouts over crust, if desired.

How to make a **perfect crust edge**

BRAID: Make ½ recipe additional piecrust. Divide dough into 3 equal portions, and roll into long thin ropes. Flatten ropes into ribbons, and braid. Use water to adhere braid to crust edge.

CUTOUTS: Make ½ recipe additional piecrust. Cut out small shapes using a small cookie cutter. Brush crust edge with water, and lay cutouts overlapping around edge, pressing to adhere.

SIMPLE FLUTE: Fold edges under, and flute edges using the thumb and forefinger of one hand to form the dough around the thumb of the other hand. Repeat around crust edge.

LEAFY VINE: Using kitchen shears, make ½-inch diagonal cuts all around crust edge, spacing them ½ inch apart. Press every other tab toward center of pie.

movable feast:
HOST A CASSEROLE SWAP!

Because they're fantastically freezable, casseroles are best made in batches—one to eat and one to freeze for later. But why keep both of those Oven Chicken Risottos for yourself when you can share with friends and vice versa?

Mix up mealtime for everyone by hosting a casserole swap. Have guests bring two dishes—one to sample and one to swap—so everyone goes home with something new. Here's how to dish it out, take it, and make it a night you'll want to host again and again.

Two weeks before:

- Send out a list of casseroles across all categories: breakfast, chicken, beef, vegetarian, dessert, etc. Ask each guest to select one, bring one hot dish to sample, the same dish in frozen form, a serving spoon, and a recipe for the dish they made.

- Buy a cute serving spoon and oven mitt as an award for the favorite casserole of the night.

TIP: *Experienced potluckers might have their own portable casserole cookware, but not everyone will be as prepared. Set all your guests up for success with this suggestion: Place two kitchen towels in a basket, put the dish on top, and add more towels on top to keep everything warm, steady, and ready during transport.*

One week before:

- Plan your menu and grocery list—think light green salads, raw veggies, and warm bread. And don't forget the drinks! Buy a few bottles of red and white wines, or create a signature cocktail—like sangria, punch, or lemonade—that'll go with anything your guests may bring.

Night of:

- Warm up the oven for the arriving casseroles, greet guests, and start swapping! Ask guests to vote for their favorite and present the award to the winner.

QUICK TIP: *While you're straightening up the house, clear out the freezer to make room for all those frozen casseroles.*

Baked Eggs with Spinach and Tomatoes, page 39

breakfast bakes

Rise and dine! Start your day with these deliciously satisfying sweet or savory reasons to get out of bed. From Breakfast Enchiladas to Praline-Pecan French Toast, these recipes ensure the first meal of the day is the tastiest—and easiest—one. Best of all, most can be made ahead, giving you time to slip back into bed while your breakfast bakes.

Sunny Skillet Breakfast

Use this recipe as a blueprint for your favorite veggies and breakfast meats. Tip: For a crispier top, transfer the skillet from the middle oven rack to the top rack during the last few minutes of baking so the top browns slightly.

3 (8-oz.) baking potatoes,
   peeled and shredded
   (about 3 cups firmly packed)*
1 Tbsp. butter
2 Tbsp. vegetable oil
1 small red bell pepper, diced
1 medium onion, diced
1 garlic clove, pressed
¾ tsp. table salt, divided
6 large eggs
¼ tsp. freshly ground black
   pepper
Garnish: fresh parsley

HANDS-ON: 15 MIN. ✦ **TOTAL:** 28 MIN.

1. Preheat oven to 350°. Place shredded potatoes in a large bowl; add cold water to cover. Let stand 5 minutes; drain and pat dry.

2. Melt butter with oil in a 10-inch cast-iron skillet over medium heat. Add bell pepper and onion, and sauté over medium-high heat 3 to 5 minutes or until tender. Add garlic; sauté 1 minute. Stir in shredded potatoes and ½ tsp. salt; cook, stirring often, 10 minutes or until potatoes are golden and tender.

3. Remove from heat. Make 6 indentations in potato mixture, using back of a spoon. Break 1 egg into each indentation. Sprinkle eggs with pepper and remaining ¼ tsp. salt.

4. Bake at 350° for 12 to 14 minutes or until eggs are set. Serve immediately. (Serves 6)

* 3 cups firmly packed frozen shredded potatoes may be substituted, omitting soaking potatoes in cold water

NOTE: *Soaking the shredded potatoes in cold water keeps them from turning gray before cooking. It also rinses off some of the starch. Drain and pat them dry, so they won't stick to the cast-iron skillet.*

mix it up

Veggie Confetti Frittata: Prepare recipe as directed through Step 2, sautéing ½ (8-oz.) package sliced fresh mushrooms with bell peppers and onion. Remove from heat; stir in ¼ cup sliced ripe black olives, drained, and ¼ cup thinly sliced sun-dried tomatoes in oil, drained. Whisk together eggs, freshly ground black pepper, and remaining ¼ tsp. salt; whisk in ½ cup (2 oz.) shredded Swiss cheese. Pour egg mixture over potato mixture in skillet. Bake at 350° for 9 to 10 minutes or until set. Cut into wedges, and serve immediately. (Serves 6)

Sausage-Hash Brown Breakfast Casserole

The frozen hash browns help make this breakfast casserole quick and easy. If you prefer a spicier dish, substitute a second pound of hot ground pork for the mild sausage.

1 lb. mild ground pork sausage

1 lb. hot ground pork sausage

1 (30-oz.) package frozen hash browns

1½ tsp. table salt, divided

½ tsp. freshly ground black pepper

1 cup shredded Cheddar cheese

6 large eggs

2 cups milk

Garnish: thinly sliced green onions

HANDS-ON: 25 MIN. ✦ **TOTAL:** 1 HR., 5 MIN.

1. Preheat oven to 350°. Cook sausages in a large skillet over medium-high heat, stirring often, 6 to 8 minutes or until sausage crumbles and is no longer pink. Drain well.

2. Prepare hash browns according to package directions, using ½ tsp. salt and pepper.

3. Stir together hash browns, sausage, and cheese. Pour into a lightly greased 13- x 9-inch baking dish.

4. Whisk together eggs, milk, and remaining 1 tsp. salt. Pour evenly over potato mixture.

5. Bake at 350° for 35 to 40 minutes. (Serves 10)

serve it on the side

Gouda Grits: Bring 4 cups chicken broth, 1 cup whipping cream, 1 tsp. table salt, and ¼ tsp. freshly ground black pepper to a boil in a Dutch oven over high heat; gradually whisk in 2 cups uncooked quick-cooking grits. Reduce heat to medium-low, and simmer, whisking occasionally, 15 minutes or until thickened. Remove from heat; stir in 2 cups (8 oz.) shredded Gouda cheese, ½ cup buttermilk, ¼ cup butter, and 2 tsp. hot sauce. (Serves 8)

Sausage, Pepper, and Grits Casserole

A breakfast take on shepherd's pie, this hearty dish uses cheese grits as a crust to seal in the savory—and sausage-y—flavors beneath.

CHEESE GRITS CRUST

1 cup milk

½ cup uncooked quick-cooking grits

2 cups (8 oz.) shredded sharp Cheddar cheese

1 Tbsp. fresh thyme leaves

¾ tsp. kosher salt

½ tsp. freshly ground black pepper

2 large eggs, lightly beaten

SAUSAGE FILLING

1 (19-oz.) package mild Italian sausage with casings

1 Tbsp. canola oil

2 large red bell peppers, sliced

1 medium-size red onion, sliced

3 garlic cloves, minced

1 (14.5-oz.) can diced tomatoes with garlic and onion, drained

¼ cup butter

¼ cup all-purpose flour

1½ cups chicken broth

1½ Tbsp. grape jelly

1 tsp. red wine vinegar

½ tsp. freshly ground black pepper

¼ tsp. kosher salt

HANDS-ON: 50 MIN. ✦ **TOTAL:** 1 HR., 25 MIN.

1. **Prepare Cheese Grits Crust:** Bring milk and 1 cup water to a boil in a large saucepan over medium heat; add grits, and cook, stirring often, 5 minutes or until thickened. Stir in cheese and next 3 ingredients; remove from heat.

2. Gradually stir about one-fourth of hot grits mixture into eggs; add egg mixture to remaining hot grits mixture, stirring until blended.

3. **Prepare Sausage Filling:** Preheat oven to 375°. Cook sausage in hot oil in a Dutch oven over medium heat 7 to 8 minutes on each side or until browned. Remove sausage from Dutch oven, reserving 1 Tbsp. drippings.

4. Sauté bell pepper and onion in hot drippings over medium-high heat 5 minutes or until tender. Add garlic, and sauté 2 minutes. Cut sausage into ½-inch-thick slices. Stir together tomatoes, bell pepper mixture, and sausage in a large bowl.

5. Melt butter in Dutch oven over medium heat; whisk in flour, and cook, whisking constantly, 4 to 5 minutes or until smooth and medium brown. Gradually whisk in broth, and bring to a boil, whisking constantly.

6. Reduce heat to medium-low; simmer, stirring occasionally, 5 minutes or until thickened. Stir in jelly and next 3 ingredients. Stir into sausage mixture, and spoon into a lightly greased 11- x 7-inch baking dish. Gently spread Cheese Grits Crust over top.

7. Bake at 375° for 20 to 25 minutes or until lightly browned. Let stand 10 minutes before serving. (Serves 6 to 8)

Sausage, Biscuit, Gravy Bake

Think you can't improve on a sausage biscuit? Think again. In this delicious dish, gravy, buttery biscuits, and sausage become one while baking.

1 lb. ground pork sausage

2 tsp. canola oil

5 Tbsp. butter

¼ cup all-purpose flour

3 cups milk

¾ tsp. table salt

½ tsp. freshly ground black pepper

Vegetable cooking spray

8 refrigerated jumbo biscuits

½ cup chopped green onions

¾ cup shredded sharp Cheddar cheese

HANDS-ON: 15 MIN.　✦　**TOTAL:** 1 HR.

1. Preheat oven to 350°. Cook sausage in hot oil in a large skillet over medium-high heat 8 minutes or until crumbly and no longer pink; remove from skillet, and drain.

2. Melt butter in skillet; whisk in flour. Whisk constantly 1 minute. Gradually whisk in milk, salt, and pepper. Bring to a boil, whisking constantly; cook 2 minutes. Stir in sausage.

3. Grease an 11- x 7-inch baking dish with cooking spray; place dish on a baking sheet. Split biscuits in half lengthwise; place 8 halves in baking dish. Top with half of sausage mixture and ¼ cup chopped green onions. Repeat layers. Sprinkle with ¾ cup shredded sharp Cheddar cheese.

4. Bake at 350° for 40 minutes or until golden. (Serves 6 to 8)

NOTE: *The longer this bake stands before cooking, the more custard-like the consistency will be.*

Grits-and-Greens Breakfast Bake

Two Southern staples—grits and greens—come together in this savory breakfast bake. You can get a jump start by making the collards up to three days ahead.

1 tsp. table salt

1½ cups uncooked quick-cooking grits

1 cup (4 oz.) shredded white Cheddar cheese

3 Tbsp. butter

½ cup half-and-half

¼ tsp. freshly ground black pepper

¼ tsp. ground red pepper

10 large eggs, divided

3 cups Simple Collard Greens, drained

Hot sauce (optional)

Garnishes: chopped green onions, chopped pimientos

HANDS-ON: 20 MIN. ✦ **TOTAL:** 2 HR., 10 MIN., INCLUDING GREENS

1. Preheat oven to 375°. Bring salt and 4 cups water to a boil in a large saucepan over medium-high heat; gradually whisk in grits. Reduce heat to medium, and cook, whisking often, 5 to 7 minutes or until thickened. Remove from heat, and stir in cheese and butter.

2. Whisk together half-and-half, next 2 ingredients, and 2 eggs in a medium bowl. Stir half-and-half mixture into grits mixture. Stir in Simple Collard Greens. Pour mixture into a lightly greased 13- x 9-inch baking dish.

3. Bake at 375° for 25 to 30 minutes or until set. Remove from oven.

4. Make 8 indentations in grits mixture with back of a large spoon. Break remaining 8 eggs, 1 at a time, and drop 1 egg into each indentation. Bake 12 to 14 minutes or until eggs are cooked to desired degree of doneness. Cover loosely with aluminum foil, and let stand for 10 minutes. Serve with hot sauce, if desired. (Serves 8)

Simple Collard Greens

HANDS-ON: 10 MIN. ✦ **TOTAL:** 40 MIN.

½ medium-size sweet onion, chopped

2 Tbsp. olive oil

1 (16-oz.) package fresh collard greens, washed, trimmed, and chopped

1½ tsp. table salt

Cook onion in hot oil in a large Dutch oven over medium heat, stirring occasionally, 10 minutes or until tender. Add collard greens, salt, and 3 cups water. Bring to a boil; reduce heat, and simmer 30 minutes or until tender. (Makes 3 cups)

Individual Country Grits-and-Sausage Casseroles

What's better than one big dish full of grits, sausage, and sharp Cheddar cheese? Ten ramekins baked with breakfast goodness. They're perfect for parties or make-ahead meals for an entire week!

2 lb. mild ground sausage

1¼ cups uncooked quick-
    cooking grits

3 cups (12 oz.) shredded sharp
    Cheddar cheese

1 cup milk

½ tsp. garlic salt

4 large eggs, lightly beaten

Paprika

Garnish: chopped fresh chives

HANDS-ON: 30 MIN. ✦ **TOTAL:** 9 HR., 32 MIN., INCLUDING CHILL TIME

1. Brown sausage in a large skillet, stirring often, 6 to 8 minutes or until sausage crumbles and is no longer pink. Drain well; pat dry.

2. Bring 4 cups water to a boil in a large saucepan; gradually stir in grits. Return to a boil; cover, reduce heat, and simmer, stirring occasionally, 5 minutes. Remove from heat; add cheese and next 2 ingredients, stirring until cheese melts. Stir in sausage and eggs. Spoon mixture into 10 lightly greased 8-oz. ramekins; sprinkle each with paprika.

3. Cover ramekins with plastic wrap, and chill 8 to 24 hours.

4. Preheat oven to 350°. Uncover and let stand at room temperature 30 minutes. Bake 45 to 50 minutes or until golden and mixture is set. (Serves 10)

mix it up

Hot 'n' Spicy Grits-and-Sausage Casseroles: Substitute 2 lb. hot pork sausage for mild pork sausage and 3 cups (12 oz.) shredded pepper Jack cheese for sharp Cheddar cheese. Prepare recipe as directed.

Country Grits-and-Sausage Casserole: Prepare recipe as directed, substituting a lightly greased 13- x 9-inch baking dish for the ramekins.

Looking to lighten it up? Substitute 2 (12-oz.) packages reduced-fat ground pork sausage for 2 lb. sausage, 3 cups shredded 2% reduced–fat sharp Cheddar cheese for Cheddar cheese, 1% low-fat milk for whole milk, and 1 cup egg substitute for eggs.

Cheddar Cheese Grits Casserole

The quick grits in this breakfast casserole cut down the cooking time significantly, but if you prefer rustic, coarse-ground grits, simply cook them according to instructions, and proceed with recipe Step 2.

4 cups milk

¼ cup butter

1 cup uncooked quick-cooking grits

1 large egg, lightly beaten

2 cups (8 oz.) shredded sharp Cheddar cheese

1 tsp. table salt

½ tsp. freshly ground black pepper

¼ cup grated Parmesan cheese

HANDS-ON: 10 MIN. ✦ **TOTAL:** 50 MIN.

1. Preheat oven to 350°. Bring milk just to a boil in a large saucepan over medium-high heat; gradually whisk in butter and grits. Reduce heat, and simmer, whisking constantly, 5 to 7 minutes or until grits are done. Remove from heat.

2. Stir in egg and next 3 ingredients. Pour into a lightly greased 11- x 7-inch baking dish. Sprinkle with grated Parmesan cheese.

3. Bake, covered, at 350° for 35 to 40 minutes or until mixture is set. Serve immediately. (Serves 6)

MASTER IT
the **FIRST TIME**

GRITS

For perfectly smooth and lump-free grits, add them to the liquid in a slow, steady stream while whisking constantly.

INSTANT GRITS

These fine-textured grits have been precooked and dehydrated. Although they take hardly any time to cook, they lack the corn flavor and have a poor consistency.

QUICK-COOKING AND REGULAR GRITS

The only difference between these types is in granulation. Quick grits are more finely ground and take about half the time to cook than regular grits. When cooked, both boast a smooth and creamy texture.

COARSE-GROUND GRITS

These grits have a more prominent corn taste and texture. They require more liquid and, therefore, take longer to cook. They are harder to find, so check with specialty foods stores or order online.

Ham-and-Cheese Croissant Casserole

The traditional ham-and-cheese croissant gets a serious upgrade with a savory sauce full of honey and mustard. Nutmeg is optional, but it adds a nice touch of spice.

3 (5-inch) large croissants

1 (8-oz.) package chopped
   cooked ham

1 (5-oz.) package shredded
   Swiss cheese

6 large eggs

1 cup half-and-half

1 Tbsp. dry mustard

2 Tbsp. honey

½ tsp. table salt

½ tsp. freshly ground black
   pepper

¼ tsp. ground nutmeg (optional)

HANDS-ON: 15 MIN. ✦ **TOTAL:** 9 HR., 15 MIN., INCLUDING CHILL TIME

1. Cut croissants in half lengthwise, and cut each half into 4 to 5 equal pieces. Place croissant pieces in a lightly greased 10-inch deep-dish pie plate. Top with chopped ham and Swiss cheese.

2. Whisk together eggs, next 5 ingredients, and, if desired, nutmeg in a large bowl.

3. Pour egg mixture over croissant mixture, pressing croissants down to submerge in egg mixture. Cover tightly with aluminum foil, and chill 8 to 24 hours.

4. Preheat oven to 325°. Bake, covered, 35 minutes. Uncover and bake 25 to 30 more minutes or until browned and set. Let stand 10 minutes before serving. (Serves 6)

Baked Eggs with Spinach and Tomatoes

Using prepared pasta sauce in this savory egg bake keeps the total prep and cooking time less than an hour. If you prefer making your own red sauce, swap out the jarred stuff for our Basic Marinara on page 16.

Vegetable cooking spray

6 Tbsp. low-fat garlic-and-herb spreadable cheese (such as Rondelé)

48 fresh spinach leaves, torn

6 large eggs

¾ cup jarred pasta sauce

6 Tbsp. half-and-half

¾ tsp. freshly ground black pepper

Toast

HANDS-ON: 20 MIN. ✦ **TOTAL:** 45 MIN.

Preheat oven to 350°. Coat 6 (6- to 8-oz.) ramekins with vegetable cooking spray. Layer 1 Tbsp. spreadable cheese, 8 torn spinach leaves, 1 egg, 2 Tbsp. pasta sauce, 1 Tbsp. half-and-half, and ⅛ tsp. pepper in each ramekin. Place ramekins on a baking sheet. Bake 20 to 25 minutes or until cooked to desired firmness. Let stand 5 minutes. Serve with toast. (Serves 6)

Bacon and Eggs Bread Pudding

Don't toss that day-old bread. Give it a second life as the base of this rich and hearty breakfast bake. It comes together in less than an hour and tastes like you've been cooking all morning.

4 large eggs

1 cup milk

⅓ cup freshly grated Parmesan
    cheese

3 Tbsp. butter, melted

1 tsp. table salt

½ tsp. freshly ground black
    pepper

⅓ cup sliced green onions
    (optional)

5 hickory-smoked bacon slices,
    cooked and crumbled

½ (16-oz.) French bread loaf,
    cut into 1-inch cubes

HANDS-ON: 7 MIN.   ✦   **TOTAL:** 47 MIN.

1. Preheat oven to 350°. Whisk together first 6 ingredients and, if desired, green onions. Add bacon and bread cubes; toss well to coat. Spoon bread mixture into a lightly greased 11- x 7-inch baking dish. Let stand at room temperature 10 minutes.

2. Bake at 350°, uncovered, for 30 minutes or until golden brown and set in center. (Serves 4 to 6)

— serve it on the side —

Diablo Bloody Mary: Place 2 cups grape or cherry tomatoes; 1 ½ cups green bell pepper, cut into 1-inch pieces; 1 cup vegetable juice; ¾ cup diced, seeded, peeled cucumber; ⅓ cup chopped red onion; 6 Tbsp. fresh lime juice (about 3 medium limes); ¼ cup firmly packed cilantro leaves; 2 tsp. paprika; and ¾ tsp. table salt in a blender and process until finely minced. Add to a pitcher with 1 cup vegetable juice, ⅔ cup vodka, 1 Tbsp. prepared horseradish, 1 tsp. hot sauce, ½ tsp. Worcestershire sauce, 1 ½ Tbsp. fresh lime juice, and ¼ tsp. freshly ground black pepper. Stir and refrigerate mixture at least 30 minutes. Serve over ice with celery sticks, lime wedges, or Spanish olives. (Serves 4)

Breakfast Enchiladas

This Mexican-inspired morning meal can be made ahead without baking and refrigerated overnight.
Let it come to room temperature for 30 minutes before placing it in the oven.

1 (1-lb.) package hot ground
    pork sausage
2 Tbsp. butter
4 green onions, thinly sliced
2 Tbsp. chopped fresh cilantro
14 large eggs, beaten
¾ tsp. table salt
½ tsp. freshly ground black
    pepper
Cheese Sauce
8 (8-inch) flour tortillas
1 cup (4 oz.) shredded Monterey
    Jack cheese with jalapeños
Toppings: halved grape
    tomatoes, sliced green
    onions, fresh cilantro sprigs

HANDS-ON: 20 MIN. ✦ **TOTAL:** 1 HR., INCLUDING CHEESE SAUCE

1. Preheat oven to 350°. Cook sausage in a large nonstick skillet over medium-high heat, stirring often, 6 to 8 minutes or until sausage crumbles and is no longer pink. Remove from pan; drain well.

2. Melt butter in a large nonstick skillet over medium heat. Add green onions and cilantro, and sauté 1 minute. Add eggs, salt, and pepper, and cook, without stirring, until eggs begin to set on bottom. Draw spatula across bottom of pan to form large curds. Continue to cook until eggs are thickened but still moist; do not stir. Remove from heat, and gently fold in 1½ cups Cheese Sauce and sausage.

3. Spoon about ⅓ cup egg mixture down the center of each flour tortilla; roll up. Place, seam side down, in a lightly greased 13- x- 9-inch baking dish. Pour remaining Cheese Sauce evenly over tortillas; sprinkle evenly with Monterey Jack cheese.

4. Bake at 350° for 30 minutes or until sauce is bubbly. (Serves 8)

Cheese Sauce

HANDS-ON: 10 MIN. ✦ **TOTAL:** 10 MIN.

⅓ cup butter
⅓ cup flour
3 cups milk

2 cups (8 oz.) shredded Cheddar cheese
1 (4.5-oz.) can chopped green chiles, undrained
¾ tsp. table salt

Melt butter in a heavy saucepan over medium-low heat; whisk in flour until smooth. Cook, whisking constantly, 1 minute. Gradually whisk in milk; cook over medium heat, whisking constantly, 5 minutes or until thickened. Remove from heat, and whisk in remaining ingredients. (Makes about 4 cups)

— *serve it on the side* —

Cilantro Pesto: Preheat oven to 350°. Bake ½ cup chopped pecans in shallow pan 5 to 6 minutes or until toasted. Cool 10 minutes. Meanwhile, place a skillet over medium-high; add 1 tsp. cumin seeds, and cook 1 to 2 minutes. Cool 10 minutes. Process pecans, 2 cups loosely packed cilantro leaves, cumin seeds, ½ cup freshly grated Parmesan cheese, ⅓ cup olive oil, ¼ cup cold water, 2 garlic cloves, 1 Tbsp. lemon juice, and ½ tsp. table salt in a food processor until smooth.

Creamy Egg Strata

A strata is a classic brunch casserole made of bread, eggs, and cheese. You can use this basic recipe as a basis for other savory options.

½ (16-oz.) French bread loaf, cubed (about 4 to 5 cups)
6 Tbsp. butter, divided
2 cups (8 oz.) shredded Swiss cheese
½ cup freshly grated Parmesan cheese
⅓ cup chopped onion
1 tsp. minced garlic
3 Tbsp. all-purpose flour
1½ cups chicken broth
¾ cup dry white wine
½ tsp. table salt
½ tsp. freshly ground black pepper
¼ tsp. ground nutmeg
½ cup sour cream
8 large eggs, lightly beaten
Garnish: chopped fresh chives

HANDS-ON: 35 MIN. ✦ **TOTAL:** 10 HR., 10 MIN., INCLUDING CHILL TIME

1. Place bread cubes in a well-greased 13- x 9-inch baking dish. Melt 3 Tbsp. butter, and drizzle over bread cubes. Sprinkle with cheeses.

2. Melt remaining 3 Tbsp. butter in a medium saucepan over medium heat; add onion and garlic. Sauté 2 to 3 minutes or until tender. Whisk in flour until smooth; cook, whisking constantly, 2 to 3 minutes or until lightly browned. Whisk in broth and next 4 ingredients until blended. Bring mixture to a boil; reduce heat to medium-low, and simmer, stirring occasionally, 15 minutes or until thickened. Remove from heat. Stir in sour cream. Add salt and pepper to taste.

3. Gradually whisk about one-fourth of hot sour cream mixture into eggs; add egg mixture to remaining sour cream mixture, whisking constantly. Pour mixture over cheese in baking dish. Cover with plastic wrap, and chill 8 to 24 hours.

4. Let strata stand at room temperature about 1 hour. Preheat oven to 350°. Remove plastic wrap, and bake 30 minutes or until set. Serve immediately. (Serves 8 to 10)

Ham and Cheese Strata

The classic pairing of ham and cheese come together in this easy breakfast strata. Serve with a side of Frozen Fruit Salad for a simple way to start your weekend.

4 **English muffins, split, toasted, and cubed**

8 **Canadian bacon slices, cut into 1-inch pieces**

Vegetable cooking spray

1 cup (4 oz.) **shredded sharp Cheddar cheese**

4 **large eggs**

8 **large egg whites**

3 cups **milk**

1 tsp. **dry mustard**

1 tsp. **Worcestershire sauce**

½ tsp. **freshly ground black pepper**

½ tsp. **onion powder**

¼ tsp. **hot pepper sauce (such as Tabasco)**

HANDS-ON: 20 MIN. ✦ **TOTAL:** 3 HR., 30 MIN., INCLUDING CHILL TIME

1. Combine muffin cubes and Canadian bacon in a 13- x 9-inch baking dish coated with cooking spray; sprinkle with cheese.

2. Beat eggs and egg whites at medium speed with an electric mixer until blended. Add milk and next 5 ingredients, beating at low speed until blended. Pour egg mixture over muffin mixture. Cover and chill at least 2 hours to overnight.

3. Preheat oven to 350°.

4. Remove casserole from refrigerator, and let stand while oven preheats. Uncover casserole, and bake at 350° for 45 to 50 minutes or until browned. Let stand 15 minutes before serving. (Serves 8)

serve it on the side

Frozen Fruit Salad: Drain 1 (20-oz.) can pineapple chunks in juice, reserving juice in a 2-cup liquid measuring cup; add water to measure 1½ cups. Combine pineapple; pineapple liquid; 3 (6-oz.) cans frozen orange juice concentrate, thawed; 1½ cups seedless red grapes, cut in half; 1½ cups sliced banana; and 1½ cups grapefruit sections in a large bowl. Pour into a 13- x 9-inch baking dish. Cover with plastic wrap; freeze 8 hours or until firm. Let stand at room temperature 20 minutes; cut into squares. (Serves 8)

King Ranch Breakfast Strata

Break this bad boy out for brunch, and let chicken, tortillas, and zesty pepper Jack cheese wow the crowd. For best results, make it the night before. In the morning, pour the remaining milk over the top, sprinkle with remaining cheese, and let it stand 45 minutes before baking.

½ (16-oz.) French bread loaf, cubed (about 4 to 5 cups)

8 (6-inch) fajita-size corn tortillas, cut into strips

2 cups shredded, cooked chicken

2½ cups grated pepper Jack cheese, divided

3 Tbsp. butter

1 (14.5-oz.) can diced tomatoes, drained

¾ cup chopped onion

½ cup chopped celery

1 (4-oz.) can diced green chiles, drained

2 garlic cloves, pressed

1 bell pepper, chopped

1 tsp. kosher salt

¾ tsp. ground cumin

½ tsp. dried oregano

10 large eggs

1 (10¾-oz.) can condensed cream of mushroom soup

2½ cups milk, divided

HANDS-ON: 40 MIN. ✦ **TOTAL:** 10 HR., 45 MIN., INCLUDING CHILL TIME

1. Toss together first 2 ingredients, and place in a lightly greased 13- x 9-inch baking dish. Sprinkle with chicken and 2 cups cheese.

2. Melt butter in a medium saucepan over medium heat. Add tomatoes and next 8 ingredients, and cook, stirring often, 5 to 8 minutes or until tender. Remove from heat, and cool 10 minutes.

3. Whisk together eggs, soup, and 1½ cups milk in a large bowl. Pour over bread mixture. Sprinkle with cooled onion mixture. Cover with plastic wrap, and chill 8 to 24 hours.

4. Pour remaining 1 cup milk over strata; top with remaining ½ cup cheese. Let stand 45 minutes.

5. Preheat oven to 325°. Bake strata 1 hour and 10 minutes or until set. Serve immediately. (Serves 8)

Brie-and-Veggie Breakfast Strata

You can whip up this hearty cheese-and-veggie strata in less than an hour. It requires chilling overnight, so plan to make it a day in advance. When you're ready to serve, simply pop it in the oven and bake.

1 large sweet onion, halved and
    thinly sliced

1 large red bell pepper, diced

1 large Yukon gold potato,
    peeled and diced

2 Tbsp. olive oil

1 (8-oz.) Brie round*

1 (12-oz.) package sourdough
    bread loaf, cubed

1 cup (4 oz.) shredded Parmesan
    cheese

8 large eggs

3 cups milk

2 Tbsp. Dijon mustard

1 tsp. seasoned salt

1 tsp. freshly ground black
    pepper

HANDS-ON: 30 MIN. ✦ **TOTAL:** 9 HR., 15 MIN., INCLUDING CHILL TIME

1. Sauté first 3 ingredients in hot oil over medium-high heat 10 to 12 minutes, or just until vegetables are tender and onion slices begin to turn golden.

2. Trim and discard rind from Brie. Cut cheese into ½-inch cubes.

3. Layer a lightly greased 13- x 9-inch baking dish with half each of bread cubes, onion mixture, Brie cubes, and Parmesan cheese.

4. Whisk together eggs and next 4 ingredients; pour half of egg mixture evenly over cheeses. Repeat layers once. Cover and chill at least 8 hours or up to 24 hours.

5. Preheat oven to 350°. Bake for 45 to 50 minutes or until lightly browned on top and set in center. (Serves 8 to 10)

* 2 cups (8 oz.) shredded Swiss cheese may be substituted.

Savory Ham-and-Swiss Breakfast Pie

Serve this savory breakfast pie with fresh sliced summer tomatoes or a simple salad.

1⅔ cups water

1 cup whipping cream

2 garlic cloves, pressed

2 Tbsp. butter

1 tsp. table salt

¼ tsp. freshly ground black
  pepper

⅔ cup uncooked quick-cooking
  grits

1¼ cups (5 oz.) shredded Swiss
  cheese, divided

8 large eggs, divided

½ lb. cooked ham, diced

4 green onions, chopped

½ cup milk

Garnish: thinly sliced green
  onions

HANDS-ON: 20 MIN.   ✦   **TOTAL:** 1 HR., 40 MIN.

1. Preheat oven to 350°. Bring first 6 ingredients to a boil in a medium saucepan; gradually whisk in grits. Cover, reduce heat, and simmer, whisking occasionally, 5 to 7 minutes. Add ½ cup cheese, stirring until cheese melts. Remove from heat, and let stand 10 minutes. Lightly beat 2 eggs, and stir into grits mixture; pour into a lightly greased 10-inch deep pie plate.

2. Bake at 350° for 20 minutes; remove from oven. Increase oven temperature to 400°.

3. Sauté ham and onions in a nonstick skillet over medium-high heat 5 minutes or until onion is tender. Layer ham mixture evenly over grits crust. Whisk together milk and remaining 6 eggs; pour over ham mixture. Sprinkle remaining ¾ cup cheese evenly over the top of egg mixture.

4. Bake at 400° for 35 minutes. Let stand 10 minutes, and cut into wedges. (Serves 8)

Tomato-Herb Mini "Frittatas"

Brunch guests will go wild for their own frittata full of eggs, herbs, and Italian cheese. Bake and watch these beauties rise to the occasion in the oven.

12 large eggs

1 cup half-and-half

½ tsp. table salt

¼ tsp. freshly ground
    black pepper

2 Tbsp. chopped fresh chives

1 Tbsp. chopped fresh parsley

1 tsp. chopped fresh oregano

1 pt. grape tomatoes, halved

1½ cups (6 oz.) shredded Italian
    three-cheese blend

HANDS-ON: 15 MIN. ✦ **TOTAL:** 30 MIN.

1. Preheat oven to 450°. Process first 4 ingredients in a blender until blended. Stir together chives and next 2 ingredients in a small bowl. Place 8 lightly greased 4-inch (6-oz.) ramekins on 2 baking sheets; layer tomatoes, 1 cup cheese, and chive mixture in ramekins. Pour egg mixture over top, and sprinkle with remaining ½ cup cheese.

2. Bake at 450° for 7 minutes, placing 1 baking sheet on middle oven rack and other on lower oven rack. Switch baking sheets, and bake 7 to 8 more minutes or until set. Remove top baking sheet from oven; transfer bottom sheet to middle rack, and bake 1 to 2 more minutes or until lightly browned. (Serves 8)

mix it up

Tomato-Herb "Frittata": Prepare recipe as directed, substituting a lightly greased 13- x 9-inch baking dish for ramekins and increasing bake time to 18 to 20 minutes or until set. (Serves 8 to 10) Note: *Mixture will rise about 1 inch above rim of baking dish.*

Spring Vegetable Frittata

Frittatas are Italian-inspired omelettes with the ingredients baked into the eggs, rather than folded inside like a traditional French omelette. Fresh veggies make this one a winning dish for a spring or summer brunch.

4 oz. fresh asparagus

½ (8-oz.) package cremini
   mushrooms, sliced

½ small yellow onion, sliced

1 Tbsp. extra virgin olive oil

½ tsp. kosher salt, divided

½ tsp. cracked black pepper,
   divided

2 Tbsp. butter

8 large eggs

2 oz. crumbled feta cheese

HANDS-ON: 20 MIN. ✦ **TOTAL:** 40 MIN.

1. Preheat oven to 400°. Cut asparagus into 1-inch pieces, discarding tough ends.

2. Sauté mushrooms and onion in 2 tsp. hot oil in a 10-inch nonstick ovenproof skillet over medium heat 4 to 5 minutes or until onion is tender; remove from skillet. Add remaining 1 tsp. oil to skillet, and sauté asparagus 2 to 3 minutes or until tender; stir in ¼ tsp. each salt and pepper. Remove from skillet. Wipe skillet clean.

3. Melt butter in skillet over medium heat. Whisk together eggs and remaining ¼ tsp. each salt and pepper. Add egg mixture to skillet. As eggs start to cook, gently lift edges of egg with a spatula, and tilt pan so uncooked portion flows underneath. Cook 2 to 3 minutes or until almost set. Top with vegetables and feta cheese.

4. Bake at 400° for 16 to 18 minutes or until slightly browned and puffy. Serve immediately. (Serves 4 to 6)

Bacon-Mushroom Frittata

The secret to a successful frittata is an ovenproof nonstick skillet, which allows the eggs to cook properly, keeps them from sticking, and makes cleanup a snap.

½ **cup sliced fresh mushrooms**

2 **Tbsp. olive oil**

1 **garlic clove, minced**

½ **(6-oz.) package fresh baby spinach**

1 **(10-oz.) can mild diced tomatoes with green chiles, drained**

3 **cooked and crumbled bacon slices**

¼ **tsp. table salt**

¼ **tsp. freshly ground black pepper**

12 **large eggs, beaten**

½ **cup crumbled garlic-and-herb feta cheese**

HANDS-ON: 24 MIN.   ✦   **TOTAL:** 46 MIN.

1. Preheat oven to 350°. Sauté mushrooms in hot oil in a 10-inch (2-inch-deep) ovenproof nonstick skillet over medium-high heat 2 to 3 minutes or until browned. Add garlic, and sauté 1 minute. Stir in spinach, and cook, stirring constantly, 1 minute or just until spinach begins to wilt.

2. Add tomatoes and green chiles, bacon, and next 2 ingredients; cook, stirring frequently, 2 to 3 minutes or until spinach is wilted. Add eggs, and sprinkle with cheese. Cook 3 to 5 minutes, gently lifting edges of frittata with a spatula and tilting pan so uncooked portion flows underneath.

3. Bake at 350° for 12 to 15 minutes or until set and lightly browned. Remove from oven, and let stand 5 minutes. Serve immediately. (Serves 6 to 8)

Muffin-Cup Soufflé

Fresh and floral, grated ginger elevates the basic bacon-and-egg dish to a whole new level. No fresh ginger roots on hand? Sub one teaspoon of ground ginger instead.

6 cooked bacon slices, chopped

½ cup chopped green onions

1 Tbsp. grated fresh ginger

¼ tsp. freshly ground black pepper

6 large eggs

4 large egg whites

1 cup low-fat milk

¼ tsp. table salt

12 paper baking cups

Vegetable cooking spray

Soy sauce

HANDS-ON: 20 MIN.   ✦   **TOTAL:** 47 MIN.

1. Preheat oven to 325°. Stir together bacon, green onions, ginger, and pepper.

2. Whisk together eggs, egg whites, milk, and salt in a medium bowl. Place paper baking cups in a 12-cup muffin pan, and coat with vegetable cooking spray.

3. Divide egg mixture among paper baking cups; top with bacon mixture. Bake at 325° for 25 minutes or until tops begin to brown. Cool on a wire rack 3 minutes. Serve each soufflé with soy sauce. (Makes 1 dozen)

─ *serve it on the side* ─

Millionaire's Candied Bacon: Preheat oven to 350°. Arrange bacon slices in a single layer on 2 lightly greased wire racks in 2 aluminum foil-lined broiler pans. Let stand 10 minutes. Top bacon with 1 cup firmly packed dark brown sugar, pressing lightly to adhere. Bake 45 to 50 minutes or until done. Cool completely (about 20 minutes). Cut into bite-size pieces. (Serves 10 to 12)

Brunch Popover Pancake

Scrambled eggs and bacon love to pair up with this "pancake," full of fresh, fruity flavors. It's light and hollow, and the batter rises or "pops over" the skillet when cooked, hence the name. Top it with a drizzle of maple syrup.

4 large eggs, lightly beaten
1 cup milk
1 cup all-purpose flour
¼ tsp. table salt
⅓ cup butter, melted
3 Tbsp. orange marmalade
3 Tbsp. butter
1 Tbsp. fresh lemon juice
1 (16-oz.) package frozen sliced
 peaches, thawed and drained
1 cup frozen blueberries, thawed

HANDS-ON: 15 MIN. ✦ **TOTAL:** 40 MIN.

1. Preheat oven to 425°. Place a well-greased 12-inch cast-iron skillet in oven for 5 minutes.

2. Whisk together eggs and next 4 ingredients in large bowl.

3. Remove skillet from oven. Pour egg mixture into hot skillet.

4. Bake at 425° for 20 to 25 minutes. (This resembles a giant popover and will fall quickly after removing from oven.)

5. Combine marmalade, 3 Tbsp. butter, and lemon juice in a saucepan; bring to a boil. Add peaches, and cook over medium heat, stirring constantly, 2 to 3 minutes. Spoon on top of baked pancake. Sprinkle with blueberries. (Serves 4)

Cinnamon-Pecan Rolls

Wake up the family with the smell of sweet cinnamon rolls baked with buttery pecans and topped with frosting. Beginning bakers take note: The easy dough rises in just 30 minutes.

1 (16-oz.) package hot roll mix
½ cup butter, softened
1 cup firmly packed light brown
  sugar
2 tsp. ground cinnamon
1 cup chopped toasted pecans
1 cup powdered sugar
2 Tbsp. milk
1 tsp. vanilla extract

HANDS-ON: 45 MIN. ✦ **TOTAL:** 1 HR., 20 MIN.

1. Prepare hot roll dough according to package directions; let dough stand 5 minutes. Roll dough into a 15- x 10-inch rectangle; spread with softened butter. Stir together brown sugar and cinnamon; sprinkle over butter. Sprinkle pecans over brown sugar mixture. Roll up tightly, starting at one long end; cut into 12 slices. Place rolls, cut sides down, in a lightly greased 12-inch cast-iron skillet or 13- x 9-inch pan. Cover loosely with plastic wrap and a cloth towel; let rise in a warm place (85°), free from drafts, 30 minutes or until doubled in bulk.

2. Preheat oven to 375°. Uncover rolls, and bake for 20 to 25 minutes or until center rolls are golden brown and done. Cool in pan on a wire rack 10 minutes. Stir together powdered sugar, milk, and vanilla; drizzle over rolls. (Makes 12 rolls)

NOTE: *We tested with Pillsbury Specialty Mix Hot Roll Mix.*

Easy French Toast Casserole

Sliced fresh strawberries and a cold glass of milk are all you need to serve alongside this sweet breakfast treat. Make sure your French bread has a soft crust so it's easier to cut.

⅔ cup firmly packed dark brown
    sugar
2 Tbsp. butter
2 Tbsp. dark corn syrup
Vegetable cooking spray
2 large eggs
1 large egg white
1½ cups milk
1 tsp. vanilla extract
¼ tsp. table salt
6 (1-inch-thick) French bread
    baguette slices
2 Tbsp. finely chopped toasted
    pecans
Garnish: strawberry slices,
    powdered sugar

HANDS-ON: 30 MIN.　✦　**TOTAL:** 8 HR., 55 MIN., INCLUDING CHILL TIME

1. Combine first 3 ingredients in a small, heavy saucepan. Cook over medium heat until bubbly and sugar dissolves, stirring constantly. Pour sugar mixture into an 11- x 7-inch baking dish coated with cooking spray, spreading evenly over bottom of dish.

2. Whisk together eggs and egg white in a shallow dish or pie plate. Stir in milk, vanilla, and salt. Lightly press bread slices, 1 at a time, into egg mixture, coating both sides of bread, and arrange over sugar mixture. Pour any remaining egg mixture evenly over bread slices. Cover and chill 8 to 24 hours.

3. Preheat oven to 350°.

4. Bake at 350°, uncovered, for 30 minutes or until lightly browned.

5. Place 1 toast piece on each of 6 plates. Sprinkle each serving with 1 tsp. pecans. (Serves 6)

One-Dish Blackberry French Toast

This simple breakfast dish is ideal for a holiday or weekend brunch. It's loaded with sugary ingredients, but you can always add a little extra sweetness with a hint of maple syrup or whipped cream.

1 cup blackberry jam
1 (12-oz.) sliced French bread
    loaf, cut into 1½-inch cubes
1 (8-oz.) package ⅓-less-fat
    cream cheese, cut into
    1-inch cubes
4 large eggs
2 cups half-and-half
1 tsp. ground cinnamon
1 tsp. vanilla extract
½ cup firmly packed brown
    sugar
Garnishes: maple syrup,
    whipped cream

HANDS-ON: 21 MIN. ✦ **TOTAL:** 8 HR., 30 MIN., INCLUDING CHILL TIME

1. Cook jam in a small saucepan over medium heat 1 to 2 minutes or until melted and smooth, stirring once.

2. Place half of bread cubes in bottom of a lightly greased 13- x 9-inch baking dish. Top with cream cheese cubes, and drizzle with melted jam. Top with remaining bread cubes.

3. Whisk together eggs and next 3 ingredients. Pour over bread mixture. Sprinkle with brown sugar. Cover tightly, and chill 8 to 24 hours.

4. Preheat oven to 325°. Bake, covered, 20 minutes. Uncover and bake 10 to 15 minutes or until bread is golden brown and mixture is set. (Serves 8 to 10)

mix it up

One-Dish Blueberry French Toast: Substitute 1 cup blueberry jam for blackberry jam. Prepare recipe as directed. (Serves 8 to 10)

Praline-Pecan French Toast

Make an early morning nod to New Orleans with this decadent take on traditional French toast, full of nutty flavors and a slight hint of spice.

1 (16-oz.) sliced French bread loaf
1 cup firmly packed light brown sugar
⅓ cup butter, melted
2 Tbsp. maple syrup
¾ cup chopped pecans
4 large eggs, lightly beaten
1 cup 2% reduced-fat milk
2 Tbsp. granulated sugar
1 tsp. ground cinnamon
1 tsp. vanilla extract

HANDS-ON: 20 MIN.   ✦   **TOTAL:** 8 HR., 30 MIN., INCLUDING CHILL TIME

1. Cut 10 (1-inch-thick) slices of bread. Reserve remaining bread for another use.

2. Stir together brown sugar and next 2 ingredients, and pour into a lightly greased 13- x 9-inch baking dish. Sprinkle with chopped pecans.

3. Whisk together eggs and next 4 ingredients. Arrange bread slices over pecans; pour egg mixture over bread. Cover and chill 8 hours or overnight.

4. Preheat oven to 350°. Bake for 35 to 37 minutes or until golden brown. Serve immediately. (Serves 8 to 10)

Creamy Seafood
Pot Pie, page 125

classic casserole favorites

You know them, you love them, and you can't imagine a month of meals without them. After decades of culinary evolution, pot pies and pasta bakes are still standing for one simple reason: They get the job done deliciously every single time. We've updated some methods and ingredients—think fresh mozzarella, haricot verts, and pancetta—but otherwise we haven't messed with perfection. There's just something so comforting about consistency.

Shepherd's Pie

The cheese-and-carrot mashed potato topping gives this traditional beefy pie a tasty twist. The carrots add just a touch of sweetness to the creamy potatoes, making them the perfect pair for this savory pie.

1½ lb. ground round

1 cup chopped onion

½ (8-oz.) package fresh
    mushrooms, sliced

1 garlic clove, minced

1 cup frozen peas, thawed

4 tsp. beef bouillon granules

½ tsp. table salt

½ tsp. dried thyme

¼ tsp. freshly ground black
    pepper

1 Tbsp. all-purpose flour

1 (14.5-oz.) can stewed tomatoes

1 bay leaf

2 Tbsp. red wine vinegar

Cheese-and-Carrot Mashed
    Potatoes

HANDS-ON: 40 MIN. ✦ **TOTAL:** 1 HR., 20 MIN., INCLUDING MASHED POTATOES

1. Preheat oven to 400°. Brown beef in a large nonstick skillet over medium-high heat, stirring often, 10 minutes or until meat crumbles and is no longer pink. Remove ground beef from skillet using a slotted spoon; reserve 2 Tbsp. drippings in skillet. Reduce heat to medium.

2. Sauté onion, mushrooms, and garlic in hot drippings over medium heat 10 to 11 minutes or until tender. Stir in ground beef, peas, and next 4 ingredients. Sprinkle flour over meat mixture. Increase heat to medium-high, and cook, stirring constantly, 1 minute. Stir in tomatoes, bay leaf, and vinegar, breaking up large tomato pieces with a spoon. Reduce heat to medium; cook, stirring often, 3 minutes or until slightly thickened. Remove bay leaf. Transfer mixture to a lightly greased 3-qt. baking dish or pan. Spoon Cheese-and-Carrot Mashed Potatoes evenly over meat mixture, smoothing with back of spoon.

3. Bake at 400° for 15 minutes or until thoroughly heated. Let stand 5 minutes before serving. (Serves 8)

Cheese-and-Carrot Mashed Potatoes

HANDS-ON: 20 MIN. ✦ **TOTAL:** 30 MIN.

1 (1-lb.) package baby carrots

1 Tbsp. butter

1 (22-oz.) package frozen mashed potatoes

2½ cups milk

1 cup (4 oz.) shredded Cheddar cheese

1 Tbsp. fresh thyme leaves

1 tsp. table salt

¼ tsp. freshly ground black pepper

1. Place carrots and ¼ cup water in a large microwave-safe bowl. Cover tightly with plastic wrap; fold back a small edge to allow steam to escape. Microwave at HIGH 8 to 10 minutes or until carrots are tender. Drain.

2. Stir in butter. Coarsely mash carrots with a potato masher.

3. Prepare potatoes according to package directions, using 2½ cups milk. Stir in cheese, next 3 ingredients, and carrot mixture until well blended. (Serves 8)

NOTE: *We tested with Ore-Ida Frozen Mashed Potatoes. Do not use refrigerated mashed potatoes.*

Baked Linguine with Meat Sauce

Get a jump on tomorrow's dinner by making this linguine tonight. Simply prepare the recipe as directed through Step 3, cover, and refrigerate. Continue with the recipe as directed—just add about 10 to 15 more minutes of baking time so it's thoroughly heated.

2 lb. lean ground beef

2 garlic cloves, minced

1 (28-oz.) can crushed tomatoes

1 (8-oz.) can tomato sauce

1 (6-oz.) can tomato paste

2 tsp. sugar

1 tsp. table salt

8 oz. uncooked linguine

1 (16-oz.) container sour cream

1 (8-oz.) package cream cheese, softened

1 bunch green onions, chopped

2 cups (8 oz.) shredded sharp Cheddar cheese

Garnish: sliced green onions

HANDS-ON: 30 MIN.   ✦   **TOTAL:** 55 MIN.

1. Preheat oven to 350°. Brown ground beef and garlic in a Dutch oven over medium-high heat, stirring often, until meat crumbles and is no longer pink. Stir in tomatoes and next 4 ingredients; simmer 30 minutes. Set aside.

2. Cook pasta according to package directions; drain. Place in a lightly greased 13- x 9-inch baking dish.

3. Stir together sour cream, cream cheese, and green onions. Spread over pasta. Top with meat sauce.

4. Bake at 350° for 20 to 25 minutes or until thoroughly heated. Sprinkle with Cheddar cheese, and bake 5 more minutes or until cheese melts. Let stand 5 minutes. (Serves 8)

— *serve it on the side* —

Squash-and-Onion Sauté: Melt 2 Tbsp. butter in a large nonstick skillet over medium heat; add 2 medium-size yellow squash and 2 medium zucchini sliced into half moons, 1 sliced onion, 2 minced garlic cloves, and sauté 6 to 8 minutes or until vegetables are tender. Stir in 2 tsp. sugar, ½ tsp. table salt, and ¼ tsp. freshly ground black pepper; sauté 2 minutes. Remove from heat; sprinkle with 2 Tbsp. thinly sliced fresh basil. (Serves 6 to 8)

Meatball Pasta Bake

The unique pairing of orange juice and fennel adds bright, fresh flavors to this meaty meal.

1 (16-oz.) package uncooked penne

1 small sweet onion, chopped

1 medium-size fennel bulb, thinly sliced (optional)

2 Tbsp. olive oil

3 garlic cloves, minced

1 tsp. fennel seeds

2 (24-oz.) jars marinara sauce

2 (14-oz.) packages frozen beef meatballs, thawed

1 cup fresh orange juice

¾ cup organic chicken broth

1 tsp. firmly packed orange zest

1 medium-size red bell pepper, chopped

½ tsp. kosher salt

1 cup torn fresh basil

1½ (8-oz.) packages fresh mozzarella cheese slices

Garnish: torn basil leaves

HANDS-ON: 30 MIN. ✦ **TOTAL:** 1 HR., 10 MIN.

1. Preheat oven to 350°. Cook pasta according to package directions; drain.

2. Sauté onion and fennel bulb, if desired, in hot oil in a Dutch oven over medium heat 8 to 10 minutes or until tender. Add garlic and fennel seeds, and sauté 1 minute. Stir in marinara sauce and next 6 ingredients; increase heat to medium-high, and bring to a boil. Reduce heat to medium-low; cover and simmer 10 minutes. Remove from heat, and stir in basil, cooked pasta, and salt to taste. Transfer to a lightly greased 13- x 9-inch baking dish. Place dish on an aluminum foil-lined baking sheet. Top with cheese.

3. Bake at 350° for 25 minutes or until bubbly. (Serves 8 to 10)

NOTE: *We tested with Classico Marinara with Plum Tomatoes.*

Sausage-and-Ravioli Lasagna

Your family will love this twist on traditional lasagna. Keep a stock of the ingredients in your pantry and fridge, and use whatever fresh veggies you have on hand to whip it up when you need dinner on the table in an hour.

½ lb. ground Italian sausage

1 (24-oz.) jar tomato-and-basil pasta sauce

1 (6-oz.) package fresh baby spinach, thoroughly washed

½ cup refrigerated pesto sauce

1 (25-oz.) package frozen cheese-filled ravioli (do not thaw)

1 cup (4 oz.) shredded Italian six-cheese blend

HANDS-ON: 25 MIN. ✦ **TOTAL:** 1 HR.

1. Preheat oven to 375°. Cook Italian sausage in a skillet over medium heat, stirring often, 10 minutes or until sausage crumbles and is no longer pink; drain well. Stir pasta sauce into sausage.

2. Chop spinach, and toss with pesto in a bowl.

3. Spoon one-third of sausage mixture (about ½ cup) into a lightly greased 11- x 7-inch baking dish. Top with half of spinach mixture. Arrange half of ravioli in a single layer over spinach mixture. Repeat layers once. Top with remaining sausage mixture.

4. Bake at 375° for 30 minutes. Sprinkle with shredded cheese, and bake 5 to 8 minutes or until hot and bubbly. (Serves 6 to 8)

NOTE: *We tested with Buitoni Pesto with Basil.*

mix it up

Shrimp-and-Ravioli Lasagna: Omit Italian sausage. Substitute 1 (15-oz.) jar Alfredo sauce for pasta sauce. Stir ¼ cup vegetable or chicken broth into Alfredo sauce. Proceed with recipe as directed, sprinkling 1 lb. peeled, coarsely chopped cooked shrimp over first layer of ravioli. Sprinkle with ⅛ tsp. paprika before serving. (Serves 6 to 8)

Note: *We tested with Bertolli Alfredo Sauce with Aged Parmesan Cheese.*

Tomato 'n' Beef Casserole with Polenta Crust

The polenta crust makes up the base of this savory beef and tomato casserole. The resulting combination is a rich, hearty dish perfect for cold winter nights.

1 tsp. table salt

1 cup plain yellow cornmeal

½ tsp. Montreal steak seasoning

1 cup (4 oz.) shredded sharp Cheddar cheese, divided

1 lb. ground chuck

1 cup chopped onion

1 medium zucchini, cut in half lengthwise and sliced (about 2 cups)

1 Tbsp. olive oil

2 (14½-oz.) cans petite diced tomatoes, drained

1 (6-oz.) can tomato paste

2 Tbsp. chopped fresh flat-leaf parsley

HANDS-ON: 35 MIN. ✦ **TOTAL:** 1 HR., 10 MIN.

1. Preheat oven to 350°. Bring 3 cups water and salt to a boil in a 2-qt. saucepan over medium-high heat. Whisk in cornmeal; reduce heat to low, and simmer, whisking constantly, 3 minutes or until thickened. Remove from heat, and stir in steak seasoning and ¼ cup Cheddar cheese. Spread cornmeal mixture into a lightly greased 11- x 7-inch baking dish.

2. Brown ground chuck in a large nonstick skillet over medium-high heat, stirring often, 10 minutes or until meat crumbles and is no longer pink; drain and transfer to a bowl.

3. Sauté onion and zucchini in hot oil in skillet over medium heat 5 minutes or until crisp-tender. Stir in beef, tomatoes, and tomato paste; simmer, stirring often, 10 minutes. Pour beef mixture over cornmeal crust. Sprinkle with remaining ¾ cup cheese.

4. Bake at 350° for 30 minutes or until bubbly. Sprinkle casserole with parsley just before serving. (Serves 6)

mix it up

Italian Sausage Casserole with Polenta Crust: Substitute Italian sausage for ground chuck and Italian six-cheese blend for Cheddar cheese.

Prepare recipe as directed, sautéing 1 medium-size green bell pepper, chopped, with onion and zucchini in Step 3.

Cheese-Crusted Pizza Pot Pies

You've never had pizza—or pot pie—like this. These cheesy mashups of pizza and pot pie will have your kids running to the table every time you serve these for dinner.

1 (12-oz.) package pork sausage links, casings removed, or ¾ lb. ground beef round

⅔ cup chopped onion

⅔ cup finely chopped carrots

½ cup chopped green bell pepper

3 garlic cloves, finely chopped

1¼ cups marinara sauce

⅔ cup sliced pepperoni

⅓ cup chopped pimiento-stuffed green olives

1 cup (4 oz.) shredded Italian cheese blend

Vegetable cooking spray

1 (11-oz.) can refrigerated thin pizza crust dough

1 large egg, slightly beaten

8 (1-oz.) slices part-skim mozzarella cheese

HANDS-ON: 30 MIN. ✦ **TOTAL:** 50 MIN.

1. Preheat oven to 450°. In a 12-inch skillet, cook sausage and next 4 ingredients over medium heat 10 to 12 minutes, stirring occasionally, until sausage is thoroughly cooked and no longer pink; drain. Stir in marinara sauce, pepperoni, and olives. Simmer 5 minutes or until thickened. Remove from heat; stir in cheese blend.

2. Coat bottoms, sides and rims of 4 (10-oz.) ramekins with cooking spray. Spoon meat mixture into dishes. Place on a 15- x 10- x 1-inch baking sheet.

3. Unroll dough on large cutting board. Cut in half lengthwise; then cut in half crosswise. Place 1 dough piece over meat mixture in each dish, overlapping rim. Brush with egg. Top each pot pie with 2 slices cheese, overlapping slightly. Bake at 450° for 16 to 20 minutes or until crust is golden brown. (Serves 4)

serve it on the side

Parmesan-Romaine Salad: Whisk together ⅓ cup fresh lemon juice, 1 tsp. Worcestershire sauce, 2 pressed garlic cloves, ¾ tsp. kosher salt, and ½ tsp. freshly ground black pepper. Whisk in ½ cup olive oil. Place 1 head romaine lettuce, torn, in a large bowl. Pour olive oil mixture over lettuce, and toss. Sprinkle with ½ cup (2 oz.) freshly grated or shredded Parmesan cheese, tossing to combine. Top with 1 cup large plain croutons, and serve immediately. (Serves 4 to 6)

Baked Ziti with Sausage

The layers of luscious, smoked-pork flavor in this bake start with a simple sauté of pancetta, or cured pork belly. Top that with crushed tomatoes, and ricotta and mozzarella cheeses—what's not to love?

12 oz. uncooked ziti

4 oz. pancetta or bacon, diced

1 large onion, chopped

3 garlic cloves, chopped

1 (1-lb.) package ground Italian
    sausage

1 cup dry red wine

1 (28-oz.) can crushed tomatoes

½ cup firmly packed torn
    fresh basil

½ tsp. kosher salt

½ tsp. dried crushed red pepper

1 cup ricotta cheese

1 (8-oz.) package shredded
    mozzarella cheese

Vegetable cooking spray

½ cup freshly grated Parmesan
    cheese

Garnish: chopped fresh parsley

HANDS-ON: 30 MIN. ✦ **TOTAL:** 55 MIN.

1. Preheat oven to 350°. Prepare pasta according to package directions for al dente; drain.

2. Meanwhile, cook pancetta in a large skillet over medium-high heat 3 minutes. Add onion and garlic, and sauté 3 minutes or until onion is tender. Add sausage, and cook 5 minutes or until meat is no longer pink. Add wine, and cook 3 minutes. Stir in tomatoes and next 3 ingredients. Reduce heat to low, and cook, stirring occasionally, 3 minutes.

3. Stir ricotta and 1 cup mozzarella cheese into hot cooked pasta. Lightly grease a 13 x 9-inch baking dish with cooking spray. Transfer pasta mixture to prepared dish, and top with sausage mixture. Sprinkle with Parmesan cheese and remaining 1 cup mozzarella cheese.

4. Bake at 350° for 25 to 30 minutes or until bubbly. (Serves 8)

Easy Lasagna

Lasagna couldn't be any simpler unless you're ordering it to go from your local Italian market. This recipe makes use of prepared pesto, no-boil noodles, and ready-made pasta sauce cutting prep time down to less than 20 minutes.

1 lb. mild Italian sausage

1 (15-oz.) container part-skim ricotta cheese

¼ cup refrigerated ready-made pesto

1 large egg, lightly beaten

2 (26-oz.) jars pasta sauce

9 no-boil lasagna noodles

4 cups (16 oz.) shredded Italian three-cheese blend or mozzarella cheese

Garnish: basil chiffonade

HANDS-ON: 15 MIN.   ✦   **TOTAL:** 1 HR., 25 MIN.

1. Preheat oven to 350°.

2. Remove and discard casings from sausage. Cook sausage in a large skillet over medium heat, stirring until meat crumbles and is no longer pink; drain.

3. Stir together ricotta cheese, pesto, and egg.

4. Spread half of 1 jar pasta sauce evenly in a lightly greased 13- x 9-inch baking dish. Layer with 3 lasagna noodles (noodles should not touch each other or sides of dish), half of ricotta mixture, half of sausage, 1 cup three-cheese blend, and remaining half of 1 jar pasta sauce. Repeat layers using 3 lasagna noodles, remaining ricotta mixture, remaining sausage, 1 cup three-cheese blend. Top with remaining 3 noodles and second jar of pasta sauce, covering noodles completely. Sprinkle evenly with remaining 2 cups three-cheese blend.

5. Bake, covered, at 350° for 40 minutes. Uncover and bake 15 more minutes or until cheese is melted and edges are lightly browned and bubbly. Let stand 15 minutes. (Serves 6 to 8)

NOTE: *We tested with Classico Tomato & Basil spaghetti sauce and Barilla Lasagne Oven-Ready noodles.*

Beef Lombardi

There's nothing fancy about this simple mix of ground beef, chopped tomatoes, noodles, and cheese, but that's why you'll love it. It's perfect to make ahead and can be frozen for up to one month.

1 lb. lean ground beef

1 (14½-oz.) can chopped
   tomatoes

1 (10-oz.) can diced tomatoes
   and green chiles

2 tsp. sugar

2 tsp. table salt

¼ tsp. freshly ground black
   pepper

1 (6-oz.) can tomato paste

1 bay leaf

1 (6-oz.) package medium egg
   noodles

6 green onions, chopped (about
   ½ cup)

1 cup sour cream

1 cup (4 oz.) shredded sharp
   Cheddar cheese

1 cup shredded Parmesan
   cheese

1 cup (4 oz.) shredded
   mozzarella cheese

HANDS-ON: 51 MIN. ✦ **TOTAL:** 1 HR., 31 MIN.

1. Preheat oven to 350°. Brown ground beef in a large skillet over medium heat 5 to 6 minutes, stirring until it crumbles and is no longer pink; drain.

2. Stir in chopped tomatoes and next 4 ingredients; cook 5 minutes. Add tomato paste and bay leaf, and simmer 30 minutes. Remove bay leaf.

3. Cook egg noodles according to package directions; drain.

4. Stir together cooked egg noodles, chopped green onions, and sour cream until blended.

5. Place noodle mixture in bottom of a lightly greased 13- x 9-inch baking dish. Top with beef mixture; sprinkle with cheeses.

6. Bake, covered with aluminum foil, at 350° for 35 minutes. Uncover casserole, and bake 5 more minutes. (Serves 6)

TO FREEZE: Prepare recipe as directed through Step 5. Wrap casserole tightly with aluminum foil, and freeze up to 1 month. To reheat, thaw in refrigerator overnight. Bake as directed in Step 6.

Pork Pot Pies with Corn Pudding Crust

Perfect for parties, these little lovelies are packed with spicy Spanish flavors. If you prefer a little more heat, replace the poblano chile peppers with a seeded and minced jalapeño pepper.

2 lb. pork tenderloin
½ tsp. table salt
¼ cup all-purpose flour
1 Tbsp. olive oil
1 large sweet onion, diced
2 poblano chile peppers, seeded and diced
3 garlic cloves, minced
1 tsp. dried oregano
½ tsp. ground cumin
1 cup chicken broth
1 (15-oz.) can black beans, rinsed and drained
Corn Pudding Crust Batter

HANDS-ON: 50 MIN. ✦ **TOTAL:** 1 HR., 20 MIN., INCLUDING CRUST

1. Preheat oven to 425°. Remove silver skin from pork tenderloin, leaving a thin layer of fat covering meat. Cut pork into 1-inch cubes.

2. Sprinkle pork with salt; dredge in flour. Sauté pork, in batches, in hot oil in a large nonstick skillet over medium-high heat 5 minutes or until browned.

3. Return pork to skillet. Stir in onion and next 4 ingredients, and sauté 3 minutes.

4. Gradually stir in broth, stirring to loosen bits from bottom of skillet. Cook, stirring constantly, 3 minutes or until mixture begins to thicken. Bring to a boil, and stir in black beans. Remove from heat.

5. Spoon mixture into 8 lightly greased 8-oz. ramekins or a lightly greased 13- x 9-inch baking dish. Spoon Corn Pudding Crust Batter evenly over pork mixture.

6. Bake at 425° for 20 minutes or until set and golden. (Serves 8)

Corn Pudding Crust Batter

HANDS-ON: 5 MIN. ✦ **TOTAL:** 5 MIN.

2 (10-oz.) packages frozen cream-style corn, thawed
2 large eggs, lightly beaten
½ cup all-purpose baking mix
¼ cup 2% reduced-fat milk

Stir together all ingredients until combined. (Makes 1 [13- x 9-inch] baking dish or 8 [8-oz.] ramekins)

NOTE: *We tested with Bisquick Heart Smart All-Purpose Baking Mix.*

Saucy Sausage Manicotti

Having a dinner party? Make individual manicotti casseroles for a special presentation. Simply spoon ¼ cup sauce into each of seven lightly greased 8-ounce shallow baking dishes. Top with two filled manicotti noodles, cover with sauce and mozzarella cheese, and bake.

1 (8-oz.) package manicotti

1 (16-oz.) package Italian sausage, casings removed

1 large onion, chopped

9 garlic cloves, pressed, divided

1 (26-oz.) jar seven-herb tomato pasta sauce

1 (8-oz.) container chive-and-onion cream cheese

6 cups (24 oz.) shredded mozzarella cheese, divided

¾ cup freshly grated Parmesan cheese

1 (15-oz.) container ricotta cheese

¾ tsp. freshly ground black pepper

HANDS-ON: 30 MIN. ✦ **TOTAL:** 1 HR., 20 MIN.

1. Preheat oven to 350°. Cook pasta according to package directions; drain.

2. Meanwhile, cook sausage, onion, and half of pressed garlic in a large Dutch oven over medium-high heat 6 minutes, stirring until sausage crumbles and is no longer pink. Stir in pasta sauce; bring to a boil. Remove from heat.

3. Combine cream cheese, 4 cups mozzarella cheese, next 3 ingredients, and remaining pressed garlic in a large bowl, stirring until blended.

4. Spoon 1 cup sauce mixture into a lightly greased 13- x 9-inch baking dish. Cut a slit down length of each cooked manicotti noodle. Spoon cheese mixture evenly into noodles, gently pressing cut sides together. Arrange stuffed pasta over sauce in dish, seam sides down. Spoon remaining sauce over stuffed pasta. Sprinkle with remaining 2 cups mozzarella cheese.

5. Bake, covered, at 350° for 50 minutes or until bubbly. (Serves 7)

⌐ serve it on the side ─

Cucumber Salad with Tomatoes: Whisk together ⅓ cup olive oil, ¼ cup red wine vinegar, 1 Tbsp. fresh lemon juice, ¾ tsp. table salt, and ½ tsp. freshly ground black pepper in a large bowl. Add 4 cups halved grape tomatoes, 2½ cups sliced seedless or English cucumber, ¼ cup chopped fresh parsley, ¼ cup thinly sliced sweet onion, and 2 Tbsp. chopped fresh oregano; toss well. Let stand at least 10 minutes before serving to allow the flavors to infuse. (Serves 8)

Southwest "Lasagna"

Tortillas and Southwestern seasonings take the place of pasta and Italian herbs in this savory, south-of-the-border "lasagna." Salsa and diced tomatoes with green chiles come in varying heat levels, so be sure to select the heat that suits your family's taste.

1½ lb. ground round

1 tsp. jarred minced garlic

1 (15-oz.) can black beans, drained and rinsed

1 (8-oz.) package shredded sharp Cheddar cheese

2 Tbsp. chili powder

½ tsp. ground cumin

1 (10-oz.) can diced tomatoes with green chiles, drained

1 (8-oz.) container sour cream

1 (16-oz.) bottle chunky salsa

6 (10-inch) flour tortillas

Garnishes: fresh parsley, sliced green onions, sour cream

HANDS-ON: 20 MIN. ✦ **TOTAL:** 35 MIN.

1. Preheat oven to 425°. Brown beef and garlic in a large nonstick skillet over medium-high heat, stirring constantly, 5 to 8 minutes or until beef crumbles and is no longer pink; drain.

2. Combine beef mixture, black beans, 1 cup cheese, and next 5 ingredients. Line a lightly greased 13- x 9-inch baking dish with 2 tortillas. Spoon one-third of beef mixture over tortillas. Repeat layers twice. Sprinkle with remaining cheese.

3. Bake at 425° for 15 minutes or until cheese melts. (Serves 8)

TO FREEZE: Bake as directed, and cool quickly to room temperature. Spoon into labeled individual dishes, or leave in baking dish, cover tightly, and freeze up to 6 months. To reheat, thaw in the fridge overnight. Bake at 375° for 1 hour or until casserole reaches 165°.

serve it on the side

Spicy White Cheese Dip: Place 2 lb. torn white American deli cheese slices, 1 finely chopped small onion, 1 tsp. jarred minced garlic, 2 (10-oz.) cans diced tomatoes and green chiles, ¾ cup milk, ½ tsp. ground cumin, and ½ tsp. coarsely ground black pepper in a 6-qt. slow cooker. Cover and cook on LOW 3 hours, stirring gently every hour. Stir before serving. Turn slow cooker to WARM. Sprinkle with 1 chopped jalapeño pepper, if desired. Serve with chips and lime wedges. (Makes about 8 cups)

Ham-and-Vegetable Cobbler

Believe it or not, this delicious cobbler makes use of frozen veggies and premade piecrusts. The secret to what makes it so yummy is using a basic, homemade roux.

¼ cup butter

¼ cup all-purpose flour

3½ cups milk

½ tsp. dried thyme

1 tsp. chicken bouillon granules

2 cups diced cooked ham

1 (10-oz.) package frozen sweet
    peas and mushrooms

1 cup frozen crinkle-cut carrots

1 (14.1-oz.) package refrigerated
    piecrusts

HANDS-ON: 30 MIN. ✦ **TOTAL:** 50 MIN.

1. Preheat oven to 450°. Melt butter in a large saucepan over medium heat. Gradually whisk in flour, and cook, whisking constantly, 1 minute. Add milk and next 2 ingredients; cook, stirring constantly, 6 to 8 minutes or until thickened and bubbly. Stir in ham and next 2 ingredients; cook 4 to 5 minutes or until mixture is thoroughly heated. Spoon into a lightly greased 11- x 7-inch baking dish.

2. Unroll each piecrust on a lightly floured surface. Cut piecrusts into 1 ¼-inch-wide strips. Arrange strips in a lattice design over ham mixture.

3. Bake at 450° for 40 minutes or until crust is browned and filling is bubbly. (Serves 6)

serve it on the side

Sweet Potato Soup: Drain 1 (40-oz.) can yams in heavy syrup, reserving ½ cup syrup. Discard remaining syrup. Place yams in a blender or food processor. Add ½ cup syrup, 1 (14-oz.) can vegetable or chicken broth, ½ cup fresh orange juice, and 1 to 2 Tbsp. minced fresh ginger. Process 2 to 3 minutes or until smooth, stopping to scrape down sides. Pour pureed mixture into a medium saucepan. Stir in 1½ cups coconut milk, 1 tsp. table salt, and ¼ tsp. ground red pepper, if desired. Cook over medium heat, stirring often, until soup is thoroughly heated. Ladle soup into bowls. (Serves 8)

Ham-and-Greens Pot Pie with Cornbread Crust

Several Southern faves—ham, greens, black-eyed peas, and cornbread—come together in these perfect little pot pies. Serve them on New Year's Day for a twist on the traditional lucky meal.

4 cups chopped cooked ham

2 Tbsp. vegetable oil

3 Tbsp. all-purpose flour

3 cups chicken broth

1 (10-oz.) package frozen diced onion, red and green bell peppers, and celery

1 (16-oz.) package frozen chopped collard greens

1 (16-oz.) can black-eyed peas, rinsed and drained

½ tsp. dried crushed red pepper

Cornbread Crust Batter

HANDS-ON: 35 MIN. ✦ **TOTAL:** 1 HR., 5 MIN., INCLUDING CRUST

1. Preheat oven to 425°. Sauté ham in hot oil in a Dutch oven over medium-high heat 5 minutes or until lightly browned. Add flour, and cook, stirring constantly, 1 minute. Gradually add chicken broth, and cook, stirring constantly, 3 minutes or until broth begins to thicken.

2. Bring mixture to a boil, and add diced onion mixture and collard greens; return to a boil, and cook, stirring often, 15 minutes. Stir in black-eyed peas and crushed red pepper; spoon hot mixture into 4 (8-oz.) lightly greased cast-iron gratin or baking dishes. Pour Cornbread Crust Batter evenly over hot filling mixture.

3. Bake at 425° for 20 to 25 minutes or until cornbread is golden brown and set. (Serves 4)

NOTE: *We tested with McKenzie's Seasoning Blend for frozen diced onion, red and green bell peppers, and celery.*

Cornbread Crust Batter

HANDS-ON: 10 MIN. ✦ **TOTAL:** 10 MIN.

1½ cups self-rising white cornmeal mix

½ cup all-purpose flour

1 tsp. sugar

2 large eggs, lightly beaten

1½ cups buttermilk

Combine first 3 ingredients; make a well in the center of mixture. Add eggs and buttermilk to cornmeal mixture, stirring just until moistened. (Makes 1 [13- x 9-inch] crust)

Pizza Casserole Deluxe

Delivery doesn't taste this good. Make two everything pizzas in one pan, and don't skimp on the fresh mozzarella for off-the-charts creaminess.

1 (1-lb.) package ground mild
    Italian sausage
2 garlic cloves, minced
1 Tbsp. olive oil
1 (26-oz.) jar marinara sauce
1 tsp. kosher salt, divided
½ medium-size red onion,
    chopped
½ medium-size red bell pepper,
    chopped
½ medium-size green bell
    pepper, chopped
½ (8-oz.) package sliced baby
    portobello mushrooms
1 cup sliced black olives
½ cup pepperoni slices, chopped
1 (16-oz.) package rigatoni pasta
3 Tbsp. butter
3 Tbsp. all-purpose flour
3 cups half-and-half
8 oz. fresh mozzarella, shredded
    (2 cups)
½ cup grated Parmesan cheese
½ tsp. freshly ground black
    pepper
1 (8-oz.) package shredded
    mozzarella cheese
8 to 10 pepperoni slices

HANDS-ON: 40 MIN. ✦ **TOTAL:** 1 HR., 15 MIN.

1. Preheat oven to 350°. Cook sausage and garlic in hot oil in a large skillet over medium-high heat 5 to 7 minutes or until sausage crumbles and is no longer pink. Remove with a slotted spoon, reserving drippings in skillet. Drain sausage mixture on paper towels, and transfer to a medium bowl. Stir marinara sauce and ½ tsp. salt into sausage mixture.

2. Sauté onion and next 3 ingredients in hot drippings 5 minutes or until tender; stir in olives and chopped pepperoni. Set aside, reserving ¼ cup onion mixture.

3. Cook pasta according to package directions in a large Dutch oven.

4. Melt butter in a heavy saucepan over low heat; whisk in flour until smooth. Cook, whisking constantly, 1 minute. Gradually whisk in half-and-half; cook over medium heat, whisking constantly, 7 to 10 minutes or until mixture is thickened and bubbly. Stir in fresh mozzarella cheese, Parmesan cheese, pepper, and remaining ½ tsp. salt. Pour sauce over pasta in Dutch oven, stirring to coat. Stir in onion mixture.

5. Transfer pasta mixture to a lightly greased 13- x 9-inch baking dish, and top with sausage mixture, packaged mozzarella cheese, reserved ¼ cup onion mixture, and pepperoni slices.

6. Bake at 350° for 30 minutes or until cheese is melted and lightly browned. Let stand 5 minutes before serving. (Serves 10)

Oven Chicken Risotto

Forget standing and stirring risotto for 30 to 45 minutes. This oven risotto recipe is so simple, you'll wonder why you ever cooked the stuff that other way in the past.

2 Tbsp. butter

2½ cups chicken broth

1 cup uncooked Arborio rice (short grain)

½ small onion, diced

½ tsp. table salt

2 cups chopped roasted or rotisserie chicken

1 (8-oz.) package fresh mozzarella cheese, cut into ½-inch cubes

1 cup cherry or grape tomatoes, halved

¼ cup shredded fresh basil

HANDS-ON: 20 MIN. ✦ **TOTAL:** 1 HR.

1. Preheat oven to 400°. Place butter in a 13- x 9-inch baking dish; bake 5 minutes or until melted. Stir in broth and next 3 ingredients.

2. Bake, covered, at 400° for 35 minutes. Remove from oven. Fluff rice with a fork. Stir in chicken, mozzarella, and tomato halves; sprinkle with shredded basil. Serve immediately. (Serves 6)

Chicken-Mushroom-Sage Casserole

Protein-filled almonds top this hearty, herby meal. Be sure to allow this casserole to rest a few minutes after baking to let the rice absorb the creamy goodness.

½ cup butter, divided

6 skinned and boned chicken breasts

3 shallots, chopped

2 garlic cloves, minced

1 lb. assorted fresh mushrooms, coarsely chopped

¼ cup sherry

3 Tbsp. all-purpose flour

2 (14-oz.) cans chicken broth

1 (6-oz.) package long-grain and wild rice mix

½ cup grated Parmesan cheese

2 Tbsp. chopped fresh flat-leaf parsley

1 Tbsp. chopped fresh sage

½ tsp. table salt

½ tsp. freshly ground black pepper

½ cup sliced toasted almonds

Garnish: fresh sage leaves

HANDS-ON: 1 HR. ✦ **TOTAL:** 1 HR., 40 MIN.

1. Preheat oven to 375°. Melt 1 Tbsp. butter in a large skillet over medium-high heat; add half of chicken, and cook 3 minutes or until browned; turn and cook 1 minute. Transfer to a plate. (Chicken will not be cooked completely.) Repeat procedure with 1 Tbsp. butter and remaining chicken. Wipe skillet clean. Melt 2 Tbsp. butter in skillet over medium-high heat. Add shallots, and sauté 3 minutes or until translucent. Add garlic, and sauté 30 seconds. Add mushrooms; cook, stirring often, 4 to 5 minutes or until tender. Stir in sherry, and cook, stirring often, 1 minute.

2. Melt remaining ¼ cup butter in a 3-qt. saucepan over medium-high heat. Whisk in flour; cook, whisking constantly, 1 minute. Gradually whisk in broth. Bring to a boil, whisking constantly, and cook 1 to 2 minutes or until slightly thickened. Remove from heat, and add rice (reserve flavor packet for another use), next 5 ingredients, and shallot mixture. Spoon into a lightly greased 13- x 9-inch baking dish.

3. Top with chicken, and bake at 375° for 30 minutes or until a meat thermometer inserted in chicken registers 165°. Let stand 10 minutes. Sprinkle with almonds. (Serves 6)

Skillet Chicken Pot Pie

Pre-packaged piecrusts and frozen hash browns help keep prep time for this hearty chicken pot pie less than 30 minutes—and in the oven and to the table in just an hour!

CHICKEN PIE FILLING

⅓ cup butter

⅓ cup all-purpose flour

1½ cups chicken broth

1½ cups milk

1½ tsp. Creole seasoning

2 Tbsp. butter

1 large sweet onion, diced

1 (8-oz.) package sliced fresh
   mushrooms

4 cups shredded cooked chicken

2 cups frozen cubed hash
   browns

1 cup matchstick carrots

1 cup frozen small sweet peas

⅓ cup chopped fresh parsley

PASTRY CRUST

1 (14.1-oz.) package refrigerated
   piecrusts

1 large egg white

HANDS-ON: 30 MIN. ✦ **TOTAL:** 1 HR., 30 MIN.

1. **Prepare Chicken Pie Filling:** Preheat oven to 350°. Melt ⅓ cup butter in a large saucepan over medium heat; add all-purpose flour, and cook, whisking constantly, 1 minute. Gradually add chicken broth and milk, and cook, whisking constantly, 6 to 7 minutes or until thicken and bubbly. Remove from heat, and stir in Creole seasoning.

2. Melt 2 Tbsp. butter in a large Dutch oven over medium-high heat; add onion and mushrooms, and sauté 10 minutes or until tender. Stir in chicken, next 4 ingredients, and sauce.

3. **Prepare Crust:** Place 1 piecrust in a lightly greased 10-inch cast-iron skillet. Spoon filling over piecrust, and top with remaining piecrust.

4. Whisk egg white until foamy; brush top of piecrust with egg white. Cut 4 to 5 slits in top of pie for steam to escape.

5. Bake at 350° for 1 hour to 1 hour and 5 minutes or until golden brown and bubbly. (Serves 6 to 8)

— *mix it up* —

Chicken Pot Pie with Bacon-and-Cheddar Biscuits: Omit piecrusts and egg white. Preheat oven to 425°. Prepare Chicken Pie Filling as directed through Step 2. Spoon filling into a lightly greased 13- x 9-inch baking dish. Cut ½ cup cold butter into ½-inch cubes. Cut butter cubes into 2 cups self-rising flour with a pastry blender until crumbly and mixture resembles small peas. Add ¾ cup shredded Cheddar cheese, ¼ cup chopped cooked bacon, 2 Tbsp. chopped fresh chives, and 1 cup whipping cream, stirring just until dry ingredients are moistened. Turn dough out onto a lightly floured surface, and knead lightly 3 or 4 times. Roll or pat dough to ¾-inch thickness; cut with a 2½-inch round cutter to form 15 biscuits. Bake Chicken Pie Filling at 425° for 15 minutes. Remove from oven, and arrange biscuits on top. Bake 25 to 30 more minutes or until biscuits are golden brown and chicken is bubbly. Remove from oven, and brush biscuits with 2 Tbsp. melted butter. (Serves 6 to 8)

ROTISSERIE CHICKEN

Carve a store-bought rotisserie chicken in six simple steps.

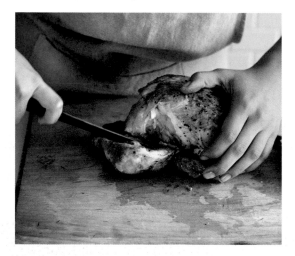

1. Place the chicken on a cutting board, breast side up. Pull the leg and thigh away from the chicken, and cut through the connective joint.

2. To separate the thigh from the drumstick, pull the drumstick away from the thigh, and cut through the connective joint.

3. Make a deep horizontal cut above each wing for easy removal later.

4. Make deep horizontal cuts along the breastbone. Use your fingers to pull away the breast meat.

5. Chop or shred the meat, or carve it in slices (shown above), starting from the outer edges and working inward.

6. Remove the wings from the chicken by pulling the wing away from the chicken body, and cutting through the wing joint.

mix it up

SHREDDED VS. CHOPPED VS. SLICED

Shredded: Meat pulled with 2 forks to "shred"

• Perfect for saucy dishes like pastas and casseroles, on sandwiches topped with dressings and sauces (like barbecue), or as a pizza topping.

Chopped: Bite-sized, cubed breast meat

• The chicken holds its shape in the finished dish.
• Use it in chicken salad or stuffed potatoes.

Sliced: Breast meat cut into ¼-inch slices

• Makes a beautiful presentation when topping a dish like pasta or to make a salad a main dish.

CHOP-CHOP CHICKEN TIPS

• **It's easiest to cut up a rotisserie chicken when it's warm.** Either cut it up as soon as you come home from the grocery store, or warm the chicken for 15 minutes in a 350° oven.

• **If at all possible, use a boning knife to break down the chicken.** The thin, narrow blade makes it easy to cut into tight spaces accurately and cleanly.

• **The average chicken yields about 3 cups chopped or shredded meat.**

Easy Chicken Pot Pie

The blend of buttermilk and white wine makes this dish the darling of the dinner table. To make it ahead and freeze, simply prepare as directed through Step 2, cover tightly, and pop into the freezer for up to a month. When you're ready to eat, remove it from the freezer, bake for about one hour and 30 minutes or until golden and bubbly.

½ (14.1-oz.) package refrigerated piecrusts

1 (10¾-oz.) can cream of chicken soup with herbs

3 cups chopped cooked chicken

3 cups frozen peas and carrots

1 cup low-sodium chicken broth

¾ cup buttermilk

¼ cup dry white wine

1½ Tbsp. cornstarch

HANDS-ON: 25 MIN. ✦ **TOTAL:** 1 HR., 20 MIN.

1. Preheat oven to 400°. Unroll piecrust on a lightly floured surface, and roll into a 14- x 12-inch rectangle.

2. Stir together soup and next 6 ingredients in a medium bowl. Pour into a lightly greased 11- x 7-inch baking dish. Top with piecrust; fold edges under, and crimp. Cut slits in top for steam to escape.

3. Bake at 400° for 45 minutes or until golden and bubbly. Let stand 10 minutes before serving. (Serves 6)

mix it up

Mushroom-Bacon Chicken Pot Pie: Cook 5 bacon slices in a large skillet over medium heat 5 minutes on each side or until crisp. Remove bacon slices, reserving drippings in skillet. Crumble bacon. Sauté 1 (8-oz.) package sliced fresh mushrooms in hot drippings 10 minutes or until tender. Add 2 minced garlic cloves, and sauté 1 minute. Prepare recipe as directed, stirring mushroom mixture and crumbled bacon into chicken mixture. (Serves 6)

Stovetop Chicken with Biscuit Topping

Perfect for topping and sopping, the biscuit "crust" on this chicken and mushroom dish steals the show.

8 frozen buttermilk biscuits

1 small sweet onion, diced

1 Tbsp. canola oil

1 (8-oz.) package sliced fresh
    mushrooms

4 cups chopped cooked chicken

1 (10¾-oz.) can cream of
    mushroom soup

1 cup chicken broth

½ cup dry white wine

½ (8 oz.) package ⅓-less-fat
    cream cheese, cubed

½ (0.7-oz.) envelope Italian
    dressing mix (about 2 tsp.)

1 cup frozen baby peas, thawed

HANDS-ON: 35 MIN. ✦ **TOTAL:** 35 MIN.

1. Bake biscuits according to package directions.

2. Meanwhile, sauté onion in hot oil in a large skillet over medium-high heat 5 minutes or until golden. Add mushrooms, and sauté 5 minutes or until tender. Stir in chicken and next 5 ingredients; cook, stirring frequently, 5 minutes or until cheese is melted and mixture is thoroughly heated. Stir in peas, and cook 2 minutes. Spoon chicken mixture over hot split biscuits. (Serves 6 to 8)

Pasta-Chicken-Broccoli Bake

Cheesy tortellini, red bell pepper, and broccoli give this kid- and mom-friendly bake a ton of flavor, while the chopped pecan topping adds a touch of crunch to every bite.

½ cup butter

½ cup chopped sweet onion

½ cup chopped red bell pepper

2 garlic cloves, minced

¼ cup all-purpose flour

3 cups chicken broth

1½ cups half-and-half

½ cup dry white wine

1 cup (4 oz.) freshly shredded
    Parmesan cheese

¼ tsp. table salt

¼ tsp. ground red pepper

1 (20-oz.) package refrigerated
    cheese-and-spinach tortellini

4 cups chopped fresh broccoli

4 cups chopped cooked chicken

½ cup grated Parmesan cheese

15 round buttery crackers,
    crushed

½ cup chopped pecans

3 Tbsp. butter, melted

HANDS-ON: 30 MIN. ✦ **TOTAL:** 1 HR., 15 MIN.

1. Preheat oven to 350°. Melt ½ cup butter in a Dutch oven over medium-high heat; add onion and next 2 ingredients, and sauté 5 to 6 minutes or until tender.

2. Add flour, stirring until smooth. Cook, stirring constantly, 1 minute. Whisk in broth, half-and-half, and white wine. Reduce heat to medium, and cook, stirring constantly, 6 to 8 minutes or until thickened and bubbly.

3. Remove from heat; add 1 cup cheese and next 2 ingredients, stirring until cheese melts. Stir in pasta and next 2 ingredients. Spoon into a lightly greased 13- x 9-inch baking dish.

4. Stir together ½ cup grated Parmesan cheese and remaining 3 ingredients. Sprinkle over casserole. Bake at 350° for 40 to 45 minutes or until bubbly. (Serves 6 to 8)

NOTE: *We tested with Buitoni Mixed Cheese Tortellini.*

Chicken-and-Poppy Seed Casserole

Forget canned and condensed soups. Our insanely easy DIY cream of mushroom soup gives new life to this comfort food classic.

2½ cups Cream of Mushroom Soup (page 15)
5 cups chopped roasted or rotisserie chicken
1 (16-oz.) container sour cream
1 Tbsp. poppy seeds
¼ cup butter, melted
18 buttery round crackers, crushed

HANDS-ON: 15 MIN.   ✦   **TOTAL:** 1 HR., 15 MIN., INCLUDING SOUP

Preheat oven to 350°. Stir together Cream of Mushroom Soup, chicken, sour cream, and poppy seeds. Spoon into a lightly greased 11- x 7-inch baking dish. Stir together melted butter and crushed crackers; sprinkle over casserole. Bake 35 to 40 minutes or until bubbly. (Serves 6)

Crunchy Chicken Casserole

Kids will love this chicken casserole topped with crushed potato chips—yes, potato chips! The salty chips add extra flavor and a crispy crunch to every bite. Be sure to add them just before baking so they don't become soggy.

2 Tbsp. butter

1 medium onion, chopped

1 (8.8-oz.) pouch ready-to-serve long grain rice

3 cups chopped cooked chicken

1½ cups frozen petite peas

1½ cups (6 oz.) shredded sharp Cheddar cheese

1 cup mayonnaise

1 (10 ¾-oz.) can cream of chicken soup

1 (8-oz.) can sliced water chestnuts, drained

1 (4-oz.) jar sliced pimientos, drained

3 cups coarsely crushed ridged potato chips

HANDS-ON: 20 MIN. ✦ **TOTAL:** 40 MIN.

1. Preheat oven to 350°. Melt butter in a skillet over medium heat. Add onion, and sauté 5 minutes or until tender.

2. Cook rice in microwave according to package directions. Combine sautéed onion, rice, chicken, and next 6 ingredients in a large bowl; toss gently. Spoon mixture into a lightly greased 13- x 9-inch baking dish. Top with coarsely crushed ridged potato chips.

3. Bake, uncovered, at 350° for 20 to 25 minutes or until bubbly. (Serves 8)

TO MAKE AHEAD: Prepare and spoon casserole into baking dish, leaving off crushed chips. Cover and refrigerate up to 24 hours. Uncover and let stand 30 minutes. Add crushed chips before baking as directed.

NOTE: *We tested with Uncle Ben's Original Long Grain Ready Rice.*

serve it on the side

Mixed Greens with Garlic Oil Dressing: Whisk together 2 garlic cloves, minced; 2 tsp. chopped fresh oregano; ½ tsp. freshly ground black pepper; ¼ tsp. table salt; 3 Tbsp. fresh lime juice; and 2 Tbsp. water in a large bowl. Whisk in 3 Tbsp. olive oil. Add 2 (5-oz.) packages spring greens mix, and toss gently to coat. (Serves 6 to 8)

Loaded Chicken-Bacon Pot Pie

Individual pot pies are great for small dinner parties. To prepare single servings, fill 6 (12-oz.) ramekins with pot pie mixture, top with puff pastry cut into circles, and bake as directed.

5 center-cut bacon slices, diced
    (about 1 cup)
1 medium-size sweet onion,
    chopped
2 garlic cloves, chopped
1 cup chopped carrots
1 (8-oz.) package fresh
    mushrooms, halved
½ cup dry white wine
⅓ cup all-purpose flour
3 cups chicken broth
¾ cup whipping cream
1½ Tbsp. dry mustard
2 tsp. fresh thyme leaves
1 tsp. kosher salt
⅛ tsp. ground red pepper
4 cups shredded roasted or
    rotisserie chicken
1 cup small frozen sweet peas
½ (17.3-oz.) package frozen puff
    pastry sheets, thawed
1 large egg, lightly beaten
Garnish: fresh thyme

HANDS-ON: 40 MIN.   ✦   **TOTAL:** 1 HR., 35 MIN.

1. Preheat oven to 400°. Cook bacon in a Dutch oven over medium heat 8 to 10 minutes or until crisp. Drain on paper towels, reserving 3 Tbsp. drippings.

2. Add onion to hot drippings, and sauté 3 minutes. Add garlic and next 2 ingredients; sauté 4 to 5 minutes or until carrots are crisp-tender. Remove from heat, and add wine. Return to heat; cook 2 minutes. Sprinkle with flour; cook, stirring constantly, 3 minutes. Whisk in broth; bring to a boil. Boil, whisking constantly, 2 to 3 minutes or until thickened. Stir in cream and next 4 ingredients.

3. Remove from heat, and stir in chicken, peas, and bacon. Spoon mixture into a lightly greased 11- x 7-inch baking dish. Place pastry over hot filling, pressing edges to seal and trimming off excess. (Use scraps to cover any exposed filling, if necessary.) Whisk together egg and 1 Tbsp. water. Brush over pastry.

4. Bake at 400° on lower oven rack 35 to 40 minutes or until browned and bubbly. Let stand 15 minutes before serving. (Serves 6)

dress it up

Guests love the layered look of a lattice-topped pot pie: Substitute ½ (14.1-oz.) package refrigerated piecrusts for puff pastry sheets. Prepare recipe through Step 2 as directed. In Step 3, spoon chicken mixture into a lightly greased 2-qt. baking dish. Place piecrust on a lightly floured surface. Using width of a ruler as a guide, cut piecrusts into 9 (1-inch-wide) strips. Arrange strips in a lattice design over filling. Whisk together egg and 1 Tbsp. water, and brush over top of pie. Proceed with Step 4 as directed.

Chicken-Chile Pot Pie with Smoked Sausage and Black-eyed Peas

Short on time? Substitute canned peas for frozen, and you will have dinner on the table in minutes.

1 (16-oz.) package frozen black-eyed peas

2 Tbsp. butter

1 lb. smoked sausage, cut in ¼-inch-thick slices

1 large sweet onion, diced

1 large poblano pepper, seeded and diced

¼ cup all-purpose flour

1 (1.25-oz.) envelope white chicken chili seasoning mix

3 cups chicken broth

3 cups chopped cooked chicken

Wild Rice Crust Batter

HANDS-ON: 40 MIN. ✦ **TOTAL:** 1 HR., 30 MIN., INCLUDING CRUST

1. Cook peas according to package directions; drain.

2. Meanwhile, preheat oven to 425°. Melt butter in a Dutch oven over medium-high heat; add sausage, and sauté 3 minutes or until lightly browned. Add onion and poblano pepper, and sauté 3 minutes. Add flour and seasoning mix; cook, stirring constantly, 1 minute.

3. Gradually add chicken broth, stirring to loosen bits from bottom of Dutch oven. Cook, stirring constantly, 3 minutes or until broth begins to thicken. Stir in black-eyed peas and chicken; bring to a boil.

4. Meanwhile, prepare Wild Rice Crust Batter as directed. Spoon hot chicken mixture into a lightly greased 13- x 9-inch baking dish. Immediately spoon Wild Rice Crust Batter over hot chicken mixture.

5. Bake at 425° for 35 to 40 minutes or until crust is golden brown and cooked through. (Serves 8 to 10)

Wild Rice Crust Batter

HANDS-ON: 5 MIN. ✦ **TOTAL:** 5 MIN.

1 (8.8-oz.) pouch ready-to-serve long-grain and wild rice mix

1 cup all-purpose baking mix

¾ cup milk

1 large egg, lightly beaten

Stir together rice and baking mix in a large bowl. Make a well in center of mixture, and stir in milk and egg just until moistened. Use immediately. (Makes 1 [13- x 9-inch] crust)

NOTE: *We tested with Uncle Ben's Long Grain & Wild Ready Rice.*

Swiss Chicken Crêpes

No time to make crêpes? No problem! Our simple solution is to use egg roll wrappers—nobody has to know you didn't work all day making them fresh from scratch.

⅓ cup dry vermouth

1 garlic clove, pressed

3 cups half-and-half

3 Tbsp. cornstarch

1 tsp. table salt

½ tsp. freshly ground black
    pepper

3 cups (12 oz.) shredded Swiss
    cheese, divided

1 (12-oz.) jar roasted red bell
    peppers, drained

3 cups finely chopped
    rotisserie chicken

1 (5-oz.) package fresh baby
    spinach, chopped

¼ cup chopped fresh basil

1 garlic clove, pressed

1 tsp. seasoned pepper

8 egg roll wrappers

HANDS-ON: 20 MIN. ✦ **TOTAL:** 1 HR., 5 MIN.

1. Preheat oven to 350°. Bring vermouth and garlic to a boil in a large skillet over medium-high heat; reduce heat to medium-low, and simmer 7 to 10 minutes or until vermouth is reduced to 1 Tbsp. Whisk together half-and-half and cornstarch. Whisk salt, black pepper, and half-and-half mixture into vermouth mixture; bring to a boil over medium-high heat, whisking constantly. Boil, whisking constantly, 1 minute or until mixture is thickened. Add 2 cups cheese; reduce heat to low, and simmer, whisking constantly, 1 minute or until cheese is melted and sauce is smooth. Remove from heat.

2. Process peppers in a blender until smooth. Pour into 4 lightly greased 7- x 4½-inch baking dishes.

3. Stir together remaining 1 cup cheese, chicken, next 4 ingredients, and 1 cup cheese sauce. Divide chicken mixture among wrappers, spooning down centers; gently roll up. Place, seam sides down, over red pepper puree in baking dishes. Top with remaining cheese sauce. Cover with aluminum foil. Bake, covered, at 350° for 15 minutes or until thoroughly heated and bubbly. (Serves 4 to 6)

Classic Chicken Tetrazzini

Casseroles don't get more classic than chicken tetrazzini. This tried-and-true chicken and pasta recipe will become a family favorite—and you'll love it for its simplicity.

1½ (8-oz.) packages vermicelli
½ cup butter
½ cup all-purpose flour
4 cups milk
½ cup dry white wine
2 Tbsp. chicken bouillon
    granules
1 tsp. seasoned pepper
2 cups freshly grated Parmesan
    cheese, divided
4 cups diced cooked chicken
1 (6-oz.) jar sliced mushrooms,
    drained
¾ cup slivered almonds

HANDS-ON: 20 MIN.　✦　**TOTAL:** 55 MIN.

1. Preheat oven to 350°. Cook pasta according to package directions; drain.

2. Meanwhile, melt butter in a Dutch oven over low heat; whisk in flour until smooth. Cook 1 minute, whisking constantly. Gradually whisk in milk and wine; cook over medium heat, whisking constantly, 8 to 10 minutes or until mixture is thickened and bubbly. Whisk in bouillon granules, seasoned pepper, and 1 cup Parmesan cheese.

3. Remove from heat; stir in diced cooked chicken, sliced mushrooms, and hot cooked pasta.

4. Spoon mixture into a lightly greased 13- x 9-inch baking dish; sprinkle with slivered almonds and remaining 1 cup Parmesan cheese.

5. Bake at 350° for 35 minutes or until mixture is bubbly. (Serves 8 to 10)

dress it up

Are those crushed kale chips on your casserole? Why, yes, they are! Preheat oven to 350°. Rinse 10½-oz. trimmed curly kale, torn into 2-inch pieces (or 14 cups), drain well, and pat dry with paper towels. Place in a large bowl. Drizzle with olive oil, and sprinkle with table salt. Toss well. Place kale in a single layer on 3 (16- x 13-inch) baking sheets. Bake for 15 minutes. Watch closely to prevent leaves from burning. Cool completely. Store in an airtight container. (Makes about 1 cup)

Chicken Marsala Tetrazzini

For in-home dining with restaurant flavors, add marsala wine and prosciutto to the traditional tetrazzini.

1 (8-oz.) package vermicelli

2 Tbsp. butter

1 (8-oz.) package sliced fresh
   mushrooms

3 oz. finely chopped prosciutto

3 cups chopped cooked chicken

1 cup frozen baby English peas,
   thawed

1 (10¾-oz.) can cream of
   mushroom soup

1 (10-oz.) container refrigerated
   Alfredo sauce

½ cup chicken broth

¼ cup marsala wine

1 cup (4-oz.) shredded
   Parmesan cheese

HANDS-ON: 10 MIN.   ✦   **TOTAL:** 45 MIN.

1. Preheat oven to 350°. Cook pasta according to package directions. Meanwhile, melt butter in a large skillet over medium-high heat; add mushrooms and prosciutto, and sauté 5 minutes.

2. Stir together mushroom mixture, chicken, next 5 ingredients, and ½ cup cheese; stir in pasta. Spoon mixture into a lightly greased 11- x 7-inch baking dish; sprinkle with remaining ½ cup cheese.

3. Bake at 350° for 35 minutes or until bubbly. (Serves 6 to 8)

serve it on the side

Orange-Ginger Glazed Carrots: Stir together 1 (1-lb.) package crinkle-cut carrots, 1 tsp. orange zest, ¼ cup fresh orange juice, 2 tsp. butter, 2 tsp. honey, 1 to 3 tsp. freshly grated ginger, ¼ tsp. table salt, ⅛ tsp. freshly ground black pepper, and 1 cup water in a medium saucepan over medium heat, and bring to a boil. Reduce heat, and simmer, stirring occasionally, 30 to 35 minutes or until liquid is evaporated and carrots are glazed. (Serves 6)

Chicken and Dressing

Thanksgiving cravings happen all year—not just the end of November. Cure them with this all-in one casserole filled with rotisserie chicken.

2 Tbsp. butter

½ cup diced white onion

½ cup diced celery

2 garlic cloves, minced

4 cups crumbled Family
    Cornbread

3 cups chicken broth

6 white bread slices, torn into
    1-inch pieces

4 Tbsp. unsalted butter, melted

2 large eggs

1 Tbsp. dried sage

1 tsp. table salt

½ tsp. freshly ground black
    pepper

4 cups shredded roasted or
    rotisserie chicken

HANDS-ON: 30 MIN. ✦ **TOTAL:** 2 HR., 25 MIN., INCLUDING CORNBREAD

1. Preheat oven to 375°. Melt 2 Tbsp. butter in a large skillet over medium heat. Add onion and next 2 ingredients. Cook, stirring frequently, 10 minutes or until softened and beginning to brown. Transfer to a large bowl. Add crumbled cornbread and next 7 ingredients. Let stand 15 minutes.

2. Spoon about one-third cornbread mixture into a lightly greased 13- x 9-inch baking dish. Arrange chicken over cornbread mixture. Top with remaining cornbread mixture. Bake at 375° for 45 minutes or until golden brown and set. (Serves 8 to 10)

Family Cornbread

HANDS-ON: 10 MIN. ✦ **TOTAL:** 55 MIN.

3 Tbsp. bacon drippings

1 large egg

1 cup milk

1 cup self-rising white cornmeal mix

½ cup self-rising soft-wheat flour (such as White Lily)

1. Preheat oven to 500°. Place bacon drippings in a 10-inch cast-iron skillet; heat in oven 4 minutes. Meanwhile, whisk together egg and milk in a small bowl. Whisk together cornmeal mix and flour in a medium bowl; gently whisk in egg mixture.

2. Remove skillet from oven; carefully pour half of hot drippings into batter. (Drippings will sizzle.) Whisk to combine. Pour batter into skillet.

3. Bake at 500° for 13 minutes or until golden brown and cornbread pulls away from sides of skillet. Cool 30 minutes. (Serves 8 to 10)

Chicken and Wild Rice with Pecans

This classic casserole is perfect for using up leftover chicken. Roast a whole chicken on a Sunday night, and then make this casserole later in the week for a quick and easy dinner with the leftovers.

1 cup uncooked long-grain and wild rice mix

1 leek, sliced

2 Tbsp. unsalted butter

1 (16-oz.) package fresh mushrooms, stemmed and quartered

½ cup dry white wine

4 cups shredded roasted or rotisserie chicken

1 cup sour cream

1 tsp. table salt

½ tsp. freshly ground black pepper

2 oz. white Cheddar cheese, shredded (½ cup)

½ cup coarsely chopped pecans

Garnish: chopped chives

HANDS-ON: 45 MIN. ✦ **TOTAL:** 1 HR., 5 MIN.

1. Cook wild rice blend according to package directions. Reserve remaining rice for another use.

2. Meanwhile, remove and discard root ends and dark green tops of leeks. Cut in half lengthwise, and rinse thoroughly under cold running water to remove grit and sand. Thinly slice leek.

3. Preheat oven to 350°. Melt butter in a large skillet over medium-low heat. Add leek, and cook 6 to 7 minutes or until lightly browned. Add mushrooms, and cook, stirring often, 15 minutes. Add wine, and bring to a simmer; cook 3 minutes.

4. Transfer rice to a large bowl. Add leek mixture to rice; stir until blended. Add chicken and next 3 ingredients; stir until blended. Transfer to a lightly greased 11- x 7-inch baking dish. Top with cheese.

5. Bake at 350° for 10 minutes. Top with pecans; bake 10 more minutes or until pecans are toasted and mixture is bubbly. (Serves 6)

NOTE: *We tested with Rice Select Royal Blend Texmati white, brown, wild, and red rice blend.*

Chicken Enchiladas

Canned green chiles give these chicken enchiladas tons of flavor, but just a touch of spice. Add some sliced pickled—or even fresh—jalapeños if you prefer more heat to your dish.

3 cups chopped cooked chicken

2 cups (8 oz.) shredded pepper Jack cheese*

½ cup sour cream

1 (4.5-oz.) can chopped green chiles, drained

⅓ cup chopped fresh cilantro

8 (8-inch) soft taco-size flour tortillas

Vegetable cooking spray

1 (8-oz.) bottle green taco sauce

1 (8-oz.) container sour cream

Toppings: chopped tomatoes, chopped avocado, sliced green onions, sliced black olives, coarsely chopped fresh cilantro

HANDS-ON: 15 MIN. ✦ **TOTAL:** 45 MIN.

1. Preheat oven to 350°. Stir together first 5 ingredients in a large bowl. Spoon about ½ cup chicken mixture down center of each tortilla; roll tortillas up.

2. Place rolled tortillas, seam sides down, in a lightly greased 13- x 9-inch baking dish. Lightly coat tops of tortillas with vegetable cooking spray.

3. Bake at 350° for 30 to 35 minutes or until golden brown.

4. Stir together taco sauce and 8-oz. container sour cream. Spoon over hot enchiladas; sprinkle with desired toppings. (Serves 4 to 6)

* Monterey Jack cheese may be substituted.

TO MAKE AHEAD: Prepare recipe as directed through Step 2. Cover with aluminum foil, and chill overnight, or freeze up to 1 month. If frozen, thaw in refrigerator overnight. Let stand at room temperature 30 minutes. Proceed with recipe as directed in Steps 3 and 4.

serve it on the side

Layered Nacho Dip: Stir together 1 (16-oz.) can refried beans and 2 tsp. taco seasoning mix; spread mixture into an 11- x 7-inch baking dish. Spread 1 (6-oz.) container refrigerated avocado dip or 1 cup guacamole and 1 (8-oz.) container sour cream evenly over bean mixture. Sprinkle with 1 (4.5-oz.) can drained, chopped black olives, 2 diced tomatoes, 1 diced onion, 1 (4-oz.) can chopped green chiles, and 1½ cups (6 oz.) shredded Monterey Jack cheese. Serve immediately, or cover and chill up to 4 hours. (Serves 8 to 10)

Creamy Tex-Mex Cornbread Bake

This one-dish turkey taco gets its subtle heat from pepper Jack cheese. Make this flavorful favorite a little lighter by swapping in low-fat soup and milk.

2 lb. ground turkey

1 cup sliced green onions

1 (10¾-oz.) can cream of
mushroom soup

1 cup milk

1 (4-oz.) can chopped green
chiles

1 cup (4 oz.) shredded pepper
Jack cheese, divided

¼ cup chopped fresh cilantro or
parsley

Vegetable cooking spray

1 (6-oz.) package buttermilk
cornbread mix

3 Tbsp. chopped fresh cilantro

HANDS-ON: 20 MIN. ✦ **TOTAL:** 40 MIN.

1. Preheat oven to 400°. Cook ground turkey in a large skillet over medium heat, stirring often, 5 minutes or until meat crumbles and is no longer pink. Add green onions, and sauté 1 minute.

2. Stir in soup and next 2 ingredients. Bring to a low boil, and remove from heat. Stir in ¾ cup cheese and ¼ cup cilantro. Add table salt and freshly ground black pepper to taste. Pour turkey mixture into a 2-qt. baking dish coated with cooking spray.

3. Stir together cornbread mix, ¾ cup water, 3 Tbsp. cilantro, and remaining ¼ cup cheese. Pour cornbread mixture over turkey mixture in baking dish.

4. Bake at 400° for 20 to 25 minutes or until golden. (Serves 6)

NOTE: *We tested with Martha White Buttermilk Cornbread & Muffin Mix.*

serve it on the side

Black Bean Salad: Cook 3 ears fresh corn in boiling water to cover 5 minutes; drain and cool. Cut kernels from cobs and set aside. Whisk together 3 to 4 Tbsp. fresh lime juice, 2 Tbsp. olive oil, 1 Tbsp. red wine vinegar, 1 tsp. table salt, and ½ tsp. freshly ground black pepper in a large bowl. Add corn; 2 (15-oz.) cans black beans, drained and rinsed; 2 large tomatoes, seeded and chopped; 3 jalapeño peppers, seeded and chopped; 1 small red onion, chopped; 1 avocado, peeled, seeded, and chopped; and ¼ cup loosely packed fresh cilantro leaves; toss to coat. Cover and chill until ready to serve. (Serves 6 to 8)

Turkey Pot Pie with Cranberry-Pecan Crusts

Fall flavors reinvent themselves under this fruity, nut-filled crust. Use different shaped and size cookie cutters to create a beautiful casserole they'll remember for seasons to come.

3 Tbsp. butter, divided

2 large sweet onions, diced

½ cup all-purpose flour

1 tsp. table salt

1 tsp. freshly ground black
    pepper

3 lb. turkey tenderloins, cut into
    1½-inch cubes

2 Tbsp. vegetable oil

1½ cups chicken broth

1 cup milk

1 (9-oz.) package fresh spinach,
    torn

Cranberry-Pecan Crusts

HANDS-ON: 20 MIN. ✦ **TOTAL:** 1 HR., 13 MIN., INCLUDING CRUSTS

1. Preheat oven to 350°. Melt 1 Tbsp. butter in a large skillet over medium-high heat; add onions, and sauté 15 minutes or until caramel colored. Place onions in a bowl.

2. Combine flour, salt, and pepper; dredge turkey tenderloin cubes in flour mixture.

3. Melt remaining 2 Tbsp. butter with oil in skillet over medium-high heat; add turkey tenderloin cubes, and brown on all sides. Gradually stir in chicken broth and milk. Bring to a boil, and cook, stirring constantly, 1 minute or until thickened. Stir in onions. Add spinach, stirring just until wilted. Pour turkey mixture into a lightly greased 13- x 9-inch baking dish.

4. Bake, covered, at 350° for 30 minutes. Remove from oven, and arrange desired amount of Cranberry-Pecan Crusts over pie before serving. Serve with any remaining crusts on the side. (Serves 10 to 12)

Cranberry-Pecan Crusts

HANDS-ON: 15 MIN. ✦ **TOTAL:** 23 MIN.

1 (14.1-oz.) package refrigerated piecrusts

½ cup finely chopped pecans, toasted

½ cup finely chopped sweetened dried cranberries

1. Preheat oven to 425°. Unroll 1 piecrust on a lightly floured surface; sprinkle with pecans and cranberries; top with remaining piecrust. Roll into a 14-inch circle, sealing together piecrusts. Cut into desired shapes with a 2- to 3-inch cutter. Place pastry shapes on a lightly greased baking sheet.

2. Bake at 425° for 8 to 10 minutes or until golden. (Makes 3 to 4 dozen)

NOTE: *We tested with Craisins.*

Baked Shrimp Risotto

Don't waste your night standing and stirring. This genius risotto comes together in minutes in the oven. Save a little cash, and swap out the shrimp for cooked vegetables or chopped rotisserie chicken, instead.

⅓ cup butter

4 garlic cloves, pressed

1 cup Arborio rice (short grain)

4 cups chicken broth

1 lb. peeled and deveined large
    raw shrimp

2 tsp. fresh thyme leaves

¼ tsp. table salt

¼ tsp. freshly ground black
    pepper

½ cup grated Parmesan cheese

HANDS-ON: 12 MIN. ✦ **TOTAL:** 52 MIN.

1. Preheat oven to 375°. Melt butter in a large ovenproof Dutch oven over medium-high heat. Add garlic, and sauté 1 minute. Add rice, and cook, stirring often, 2 minutes or until rice is toasted. Stir in chicken broth. Bring to a boil; cover and bake at 375° for 25 minutes or until liquid is almost absorbed.

2. Remove from oven. Stir in shrimp; cover and bake 5 more minutes. Remove from oven, and let stand, covered, 10 minutes.

3. Uncover; stir in thyme, salt, and pepper. Sprinkle with cheese. (Serves 4)

serve it on the side

Spinach-Grape Chopped Salad: Coarsely chop 1 (6-oz.) package fresh baby spinach and 1 cup seedless red grapes; toss with ¼ cup crumbled feta cheese and ¼ cup bottled raspberry-walnut vinaigrette. Sprinkle with ¼ cup toasted chopped walnuts. Serve immediately. (Serves 4)

New Tuna Casserole

Mom's old standby tuna casserole goes gourmet with the simple addition of mushrooms, fresh herbs, and haricot verts.

1 (16-oz.) package uncooked ziti
    pasta
2 medium leeks, sliced
1 (8-oz.) package haricots verts
    (French green beans), cut
    into 1-inch pieces
6 Tbsp. butter, divided
2 (4-oz.) packages fresh
    gourmet mushroom blend
¼ cup all-purpose flour
3 cups heavy cream
1 cup organic vegetable broth
2 cups (8 oz.) shredded sharp
    white Cheddar cheese
6 Tbsp. grated Parmesan
    cheese, divided
¾ tsp. kosher salt
½ tsp. freshly ground black
    pepper
1 (12-oz.) can solid white tuna in
    spring water, drained
2 Tbsp. chopped fresh chives
1 Tbsp. chopped fresh tarragon
    or parsley
¼ cup crushed potato chips
¼ cup panko (Japanese
    breadcrumbs)
2 Tbsp. butter, melted
Garnish: sliced fresh chives

HANDS-ON: 35 MIN. ✦ **TOTAL:** 1 HR., 30 MIN.

1. Preheat oven to 350°. Cook pasta according to package directions.

2. Remove and discard root ends and dark green tops of leeks. Cut in half lengthwise, and rinse thoroughly under cold running water to remove grit and sand. Thinly slice leeks.

3. Meanwhile, cook green beans in boiling salted water to cover 30 seconds to 1 minute or until crisp-tender; drain. Plunge into ice water to stop the cooking process; drain.

4. Melt 2 Tbsp. butter in a large skillet over medium-high heat. Add leeks, and sauté 2 minutes; add mushrooms, and sauté 5 minutes or until lightly browned. Transfer leek mixture to a small bowl. Wipe skillet clean.

5. Melt remaining 4 Tbsp. butter in skillet over medium heat; whisk in flour, and cook, whisking constantly, 2 minutes. Gradually whisk in cream and broth. Bring mixture to a boil, stirring often. Reduce heat to medium-low; gradually whisk in Cheddar cheese and 4 Tbsp. Parmesan cheese until smooth. Stir in salt and pepper.

6. Stir cream mixture into pasta. Stir in tuna, next 2 ingredients, green beans, and leek mixture; transfer to a lightly greased 13- x 9-inch baking dish.

7. Stir together potato chips, next 2 ingredients, and remaining 2 Tbsp. Parmesan cheese in a small bowl; sprinkle over pasta mixture.

8. Bake at 350° for 35 to 40 minutes or until bubbly. Let stand 5 minutes before serving. (Serves 8)

Cajun Shrimp Casserole

This seafood casserole gets its Cajun flair from the addition of okra, bell peppers, and ground red pepper.

2 lb. unpeeled, large fresh
    shrimp
¼ cup butter
1 small red onion, chopped
½ cup chopped red bell pepper
½ cup chopped yellow bell
    pepper
½ cup chopped green bell
    pepper
4 garlic cloves, minced
2 cups fresh or frozen sliced
    okra
1 Tbsp. fresh lemon juice
1½ tsp. table salt
1 (10¾-oz.) can cream of shrimp
    or mushroom soup
½ cup dry white wine
1 Tbsp. soy sauce
½ tsp. ground red pepper
3 cups cooked long-grain rice
¼ cup grated Parmesan cheese
Garnishes: quartered lemon
    wedges

HANDS-ON: 30 MIN. ✦ **TOTAL:** 1 HR., 6 MIN.

1. Preheat oven to 350°. Peel shrimp; devein, if desired.

2. Melt ¼ cup butter in large skillet over medium-high heat. Add onion and next 3 ingredients; sauté 7 minutes or until tender. Add garlic, and sauté 1 minute. Stir in okra, lemon juice, and salt; sauté 5 minutes. Add shrimp, and cook 3 minutes or until shrimp turn pink. Stir in soup and next 4 ingredients until blended. Pour into a lightly greased 11- x 7-inch baking dish. Sprinkle evenly with Parmesan cheese.

3. Bake at 350° for 15 to 20 minutes or until casserole is bubbly and cheese is lightly browned. (Serves 6)

dress it up

Crush homemade Cajun tortilla chips on top for extra crunch and kick. Preheat oven to 375°. Combine 1½ tsp. paprika, 1 tsp. dried thyme, ½ tsp. garlic powder, ½ tsp. onion powder, ½ tsp. freshly ground black pepper, ¼ tsp. table salt, ¼ tsp. sugar, and ¼ tsp. ground red pepper in a small bowl. Arrange 10 (7-inch) flour tortillas, cut into 8 wedges, on 2 baking sheets coated with cooking spray. Coat wedges with cooking spray and sprinkle with 2 tsp. Cajun seasoning. Bake for 6 minutes or until crisp.

Creamy Seafood Pot Pie *(pictured on page 66)*

This rich seafood pot pie pairs well with a salad of bitter greens and applewood smoked bacon tossed in a bright citrus vinaigrette.

½ cup butter

1 sweet potato, cubed

2 small leeks, white parts with 1 inch of green, chopped

1 cup chopped celery

1 Tbsp. chopped fresh thyme

3 garlic cloves, minced

½ cup all-purpose flour

4 cups milk

1½ lb. cod or halibut fillet, cut into 2-inch cubes

1½ cups halved green beans or haricots verts (French green beans), blanched

1½ tsp. table salt

½ tsp. freshly ground black pepper

1 (17.3-oz.) package frozen puff pastry sheets, thawed

1 large egg yolk

HANDS-ON: 25 MIN. ✦ **TOTAL:** 42 MIN.

1. Preheat oven to 400°. Melt butter over medium-high heat in a large Dutch oven. Sauté potato, leeks, and celery for 10 minutes. Add thyme and garlic; cook 1 minute. Sprinkle flour over vegetables, and cook, stirring constantly, 3 minutes. Whisk in milk; bring to a boil. Reduce heat to low, and simmer 2 to 3 minutes or until potato is almost tender. Add cod and next 3 ingredients; return mixture to a simmer. Remove from heat. (Fish will be undercooked.) Ladle filling into 4 to 6 individual ovenproof soup crocks.

2. Roll out pastry on a lightly floured surface until smooth. Cut pastry into circles, cutting the circles 1 inch larger than the mouth of the soup crocks. Whisk together egg yolk and 1 Tbsp. water; brush underside of pastry edges with egg wash and place over crock, pressing edges to seal. Brush tops with egg wash. Place crocks on baking sheet. Bake at 400° for 14 to 16 minutes or until pastry is golden brown. (Serves 4 to 6)

Crawfish Pies

If you're a fan of the Louisiana lobster, you'll love this pot pie because all of the hard work is done for you! The best part about this recipe is it makes enough for two pies, so you can make one for tonight's dinner and one to freeze for later.

2 Tbsp. butter

2 Tbsp. olive oil

1¾ cups diced green bell pepper

1 cup diced white onion

½ cup diced celery

¼ cup chopped green onions

8 garlic cloves, chopped

1½ Tbsp. cornstarch

1 (5-oz.) can evaporated milk

3 lb. peeled crawfish tails*

1 (10.75-oz.) can cream of
    mushroom soup

1 Tbsp. Cajun seasoning

½ tsp. table salt

1 tsp. freshly ground black
    pepper

2 (14.1-oz.) packages refrigerated
    piecrusts

1 large egg, lightly beaten

HANDS-ON: 30 MIN.   ✦   **TOTAL:** 1 HR., 45 MIN.

1. Preheat oven to 350°. Melt butter with olive oil in a large cast-iron skillet over high heat. Add bell pepper and next 3 ingredients; cook, stirring occasionally, 8 minutes or until tender and starting to brown. Add garlic; cook 1 minute.

2. Mix cornstarch with evaporated milk; add to skillet. Reduce heat to medium. Stir in crawfish and cream of mushroom soup; cook, stirring constantly, 3 minutes or until thickened. Remove from heat; stir in Cajun seasoning, salt, and pepper.

3. Fit 1 piecrust into each of 2 (9-inch) pie plates. Prick bottom and sides of piecrusts with a fork. Divide crawfish mixture between pies. Cover with remaining piecrusts; fold edges under, and crimp, sealing to bottom crust. Cut slits in top for steam to escape. Brush piecrusts with egg.

4. Bake at 350° for 45 minutes or until golden brown. Let stand 30 minutes before serving. (Makes 2 [9-inch] pies, 8 servings each)

* Frozen precooked crawfish tails or peeled shrimp may be substituted.

Blue Crab Casserole

Turn a weeknight dinner into a special occasion with this rich seafood dish dressed in white wine, cream, and a few shakes of hot sauce.

1 (1-inch) slice fresh challah
    bread or 1 (2-inch) slice
    French bread
2 Tbsp. unsalted butter
1½ cups diced Vidalia onion
½ cup diced celery
½ cup chopped green onions
¼ cup diced red bell pepper
2 cups fresh corn kernels
    (4 ears)
½ cup dry white wine
1¼ cups heavy cream
1 lb. fresh lump blue crabmeat,
    picked and drained
1 Tbsp. chopped fresh parsley
2 Tbsp. fresh lemon juice
½ tsp. table salt
½ tsp. hot sauce
¼ tsp. freshly ground black
    pepper
2 Tbsp. unsalted butter, melted

HANDS-ON: 35 MIN. ✦ **TOTAL:** 55 MIN.

1. Preheat oven to 350°. Process bread in a food processor until finely crumbled. (You should have ¾ cup breadcrumbs.) Set aside.

2. Melt 2 Tbsp. butter in a large skillet over medium heat. Add onion and next 3 ingredients. Cook, stirring often, 6 minutes. Add corn, and cook, stirring often, 4 minutes or until lightly browned. Stir in wine; cook 2 minutes or until wine has almost completely evaporated. Add cream; cook 4 minutes or until slightly thickened. Stir in crab and next 5 ingredients. Cook 2 minutes. Pour into a lightly greased 8-inch square baking dish.

3. Toss breadcrumbs with 2 Tbsp. melted butter, and sprinkle over top of crab mixture. Bake at 350° for 20 minutes or until lightly browned and bubbly. (Serves 6 to 10)

serve it on the side

Herbed Peas and Onions: Sauté 1 cup sliced onion in 1 Tbsp. hot oil in a large skillet over medium-high heat 5 minutes or until tender. Add 1 (14.4-oz.) bag frozen sweet peas; cook, stirring occasionally, 3 minutes or until peas are thoroughly heated. Remove from heat; stir in ¼ cup chopped fresh basil or mint, 1 tsp. lemon zest, ½ tsp. table salt, and ½ tsp. freshly ground black pepper. (Serves 6)

Cheesy Broccoli-and-Rice Casserole, page 148

chapter 3

meatless mains

Can food be filling and flavorful without meat? Kale yes! Beans, lentils, and cheese pack in the protein while mushrooms, broccoli, and gorgeous greens work their magic on your tongue and in your body. From pot pies and lasagnas to enchiladas and savory bread puddings, it's high time your favorite farmers' market finds became the stars of the show.

Eggplant Parmesan Lasagna

Bitterness be gone! Slice eggplant, sprinkle with salt, and place it on layers of paper towels for 10 minutes to rid it of excess moisture and bitterness.

2 (26-oz.) jars tomato, garlic,
    and onion pasta sauce
¼ cup chopped fresh basil
½ tsp. dried crushed red pepper
½ cup whipping cream
1 cup grated Parmesan cheese
1 large eggplant (about 1½ lb.)
½ tsp. table salt
¼ tsp. freshly ground black
    pepper
3 large eggs, lightly beaten
1 cup all-purpose flour
6 Tbsp. olive oil
6 lasagna noodles, cooked and
    drained
1 (15-oz.) container low-fat
    ricotta cheese
2 cups (8 oz.) shredded
    mozzarella cheese
Garnish: fresh basil leaves

HANDS-ON: 1 HR., 10 MIN. ✦ **TOTAL:** 2 HR., 35 MIN.

1. Preheat oven to 350°. Cook first 3 ingredients in a 3½-qt. saucepan over medium-low heat 30 minutes. Remove from heat; stir in cream and Parmesan cheese. Set aside.

2. Peel eggplant, and cut crosswise into ¼-inch-thick slices. Sprinkle slices evenly with salt and black pepper. Stir together eggs and 3 Tbsp. water. Dredge eggplant in flour; dip into egg mixture, and dredge again in flour, shaking off excess.

3. Cook eggplant, in batches, in 1½ Tbsp. hot oil in a large nonstick skillet over medium-high heat 4 minutes on each side or until golden brown and slightly softened. Drain on paper towels. Repeat with remaining oil and eggplant, wiping skillet clean after each batch, if necessary.

4. Layer 3 lasagna noodles lengthwise in a lightly greased 13- x 9-inch baking dish. Top with one-third tomato sauce mixture and half of eggplant. Dollop half of ricotta cheese on eggplant; top with half of mozzarella. Repeat layers with remaining noodles, one-third sauce mixture, remaining eggplant, and remaining ricotta. Top with remaining one-third sauce mixture and mozzarella cheese.

5. Bake at 350° for 35 to 40 minutes or until golden brown. Let stand 20 minutes before serving. (Serves 8 to 10)

NOTE: *We tested with Classico Organic Tomato, Herbs & Spices Pasta Sauce.*

Eggplant Parmesan with Feta

This take on traditional eggplant Parm is roasted rather than fried, and it replaces creamy mozzerella with tangier cottage and feta cheeses.

½ small eggplant
¾ tsp. table salt, divided
1 tsp. freshly ground black
    pepper, divided
1 cup Italian breadcrumbs
½ cup grated Parmesan cheese,
    divided
3 large eggs, lightly beaten
Vegetable cooking spray
1 medium onion, chopped
2 garlic cloves, minced
1 (28-oz.) can crushed tomatoes
1 tsp. sugar
1 tsp. dried basil
½ tsp. dried oregano
1 (16-oz.) container 1% low-fat
    cottage cheese
½ cup crumbled feta cheese

HANDS-ON: 50 MIN. ✦ **TOTAL:** 1 HR., 46 MIN.

1. Preheat oven to 375°. Cut eggplant crosswise into ⅛-inch-thick slices. Sprinkle evenly with ½ tsp. salt and ½ tsp. pepper.

2. Combine breadcrumbs and 3 Tbsp. Parmesan cheese. Stir together eggs and 3 Tbsp. water. Dip eggplant into egg mixture; dredge in breadcrumb mixture. Coat eggplant evenly on both sides with cooking spray. Arrange slices on an oven rack coated with cooking spray; place rack inside a roasting pan.

3. Bake at 375° for 16 minutes, turning after 8 minutes. Reduce oven temperature to 350°.

4. Sauté chopped onion and garlic in a large saucepan coated with cooking spray over medium-high heat 5 minutes or until onion is tender. Add tomatoes, remaining ¼ tsp. salt, remaining ½ tsp. pepper, sugar, basil, and oregano; bring to a boil. Reduce heat, and simmer, stirring often, 10 minutes or until thickened.

5. Spoon 1 cup tomato mixture into an 8-inch square baking dish coated with cooking spray; arrange one-third of eggplant slices in a single layer over tomato mixture.

6. Stir together cottage cheese and feta cheese; spoon ⅓ cup cheese mixture over eggplant. Spoon 1 cup tomato mixture over cheese mixture. Repeat layers twice, ending with tomato mixture. Sprinkle with remaining Parmesan cheese.

7. Bake at 350° for 35 to 40 minutes or until bubbly and golden brown. (Serves 6)

serve it on the side

Olive Tapenade: In food processor, place 1 cup pimiento-stuffed green olives, ½ cup pitted kalamata olives, ¼ cup chopped fresh flat-leaf parsley, 3 Tbsp. olive oil, 1 tsp. herbes de Provence, 2 tsp. fresh lemon juice, and ½ tsp. freshly ground black pepper. Process using quick on-and-off motions, just until olives are coarsely chopped. Spoon spread into serving bowl. Stir in 1 Tbsp. drained capers. Serve immediately with bakery-style bread or crackers. (Serves 13)

Fresh Vegetable Lasagna

Veggie lasagna is ideal for utilizing everything from zucchini and mushrooms to red and yellow bell peppers.

4 medium zucchini, halved
   lengthwise and thinly sliced
1 (8-oz.) package sliced fresh
   mushrooms
2 garlic cloves, minced
Vegetable cooking spray
1 medium-size red bell pepper,
   chopped
1 medium-size yellow bell
   pepper, chopped
1 yellow onion, chopped
½ tsp. table salt
1½ cups ricotta cheese
1 large egg
2 cups (8 oz.) shredded part-
   skim mozzarella cheese,
   divided
½ cup freshly grated Parmesan
   cheese, divided
5 cups Basic Marinara (page 16)
1 (8-oz.) package no-boil lasagna
   noodles
Garnish: fresh basil leaves

HANDS-ON: 30 MIN. ✦ **TOTAL:** 3 HR., 14 MIN., INCLUDING SAUCE

1. Preheat oven to 450°. Place zucchini, mushrooms, and garlic in a jelly-roll pan coated with cooking spray. Bake for 12 to 14 minutes or until vegetables are crisp-tender, stirring halfway through. Repeat procedure with bell peppers and onion. Reduce oven temperature to 350°. Toss together vegetables and salt in a bowl.

2. Stir together ricotta, egg, 1½ cups shredded mozzarella cheese, and ¼ cup grated Parmesan cheese.

3. Spread 1 cup Basic Marinara in a 13- x 9-inch baking dish coated with cooking spray. Top with 3 noodles, 1 cup sauce, one-third of ricotta mixture, and one-third of vegetable mixture; repeat layers twice, beginning with 3 noodles. Top with remaining noodles and 1 cup sauce. Sprinkle with remaining ½ cup shredded mozzarella and ¼ cup grated Parmesan.

4. Bake, covered, at 350° for 45 minutes. Uncover and bake 10 to 15 more minutes or until cheese is melted and golden. Let stand 10 minutes. (Serves 8)

Tomato-Basil Lasagna Rolls

Baby artichokes add taste and texture to this fun twist on layered lasagna.

10 uncooked lasagna noodles

1 cup finely chopped sweet
    onion

2 tsp. olive oil

3 garlic cloves, minced and
    divided

1 (24-oz.) jar tomato-and-basil
    pasta sauce

1½ tsp. sugar

¼ tsp. dried crushed red pepper

1 cup low-fat ricotta cheese

2 oz. ⅓-less-fat cream cheese,
    softened

1 (14-oz.) can baby artichoke
    hearts, drained and
    quartered

1 large egg white, lightly beaten

¼ cup torn fresh basil

¼ cup (1 oz.) freshly shredded
    Parmesan cheese

Toppings: fresh basil, Parmesan
    cheese

HANDS-ON: 35 MIN. ✦ **TOTAL:** 1 HR., 35 MIN.

1. Preheat oven to 350°. Cook pasta according to package directions for al dente. Drain pasta (do not rinse); arrange in a single layer on lightly greased aluminum foil.

2. Sauté onion in hot oil in a 3-qt. saucepan over medium heat 7 to 8 minutes or until caramelized. Add two-thirds of minced garlic, and cook, stirring constantly, 1 minute. Stir in pasta sauce and next 2 ingredients. Bring mixture to a boil, stirring often. Reduce heat to low; simmer, stirring often, 5 minutes. Remove from heat.

3. Stir together ricotta and cream cheese until smooth. Stir in artichoke hearts, next 3 ingredients, and remaining minced garlic. Spread ¼ cup cheese mixture on 1 noodle. Roll up firmly, and place, seam side down, into a lightly greased 11- x 7-inch baking dish. Repeat with remaining noodles and cheese. Spoon pasta sauce mixture over lasagna rolls.

4. Bake, covered, at 350° for 45 to 50 minutes or until thoroughly heated and bubbly. Let stand 5 minutes. Sprinkle with desired toppings. (Serves 10)

NOTE: *We tested with Classico Tomato & Basil pasta sauce.*

dress it up

Parmesan crisps add the elegant look of lace to the top of any casserole. Preheat oven to 350°. Sprinkle about 1 Tbsp. finely shredded Parmesan cheese, forming a 2-inch round, on an aluminum-foil lined baking sheet coated with cooking spray. Repeat with 1½ cups cheese, leaving 1 inch between rounds. Bake at 350° for 8 minutes or until lightly browned. Quickly remove cheese crisps from baking sheet with a spatula. Cool on a wire rack. Store in an airtight container. (Makes 2 dozen)

Spinach-Ravioli Bake

Pasta meets pesto in this simple ravioli bake filled with greens galore.

**1 (6-oz.) package fresh baby
  spinach, thoroughly washed**
⅓ cup refrigerated pesto sauce
1 (15-oz.) jar Alfredo sauce
¼ cup vegetable broth
**1 (25-oz.) package frozen cheese-
  filled ravioli (do not thaw)**
**1 cup (4 oz.) shredded Italian
  six-cheese blend**

HANDS-ON: 15 MIN. ✦ **TOTAL:** 50 MIN.

1. Preheat oven to 375°. Chop spinach, and toss with pesto in a medium bowl.

2. Combine Alfredo sauce and vegetable broth. Spoon one-third of Alfredo sauce mixture (about ½ cup) into a lightly greased 2.2-qt. or 11- x 7-inch baking dish. Top with half of spinach mixture. Arrange half of ravioli in a single layer over spinach mixture. Repeat layers once. Top with remaining Alfredo sauce.

3. Bake at 375° for 30 minutes. Remove from oven, and sprinkle with shredded cheese. Bake 5 more minutes or until hot and bubbly. (Serves 6 to 8)

serve it on the side

Tomato, Watermelon, and Feta Skewers with Mint and Lime: Gently toss together 2 large heirloom tomatoes (cored and cut into 1-inch pieces), 3 cups 1-inch watermelon cubes, 8 oz. feta cheese (cubed), 2½ Tbsp. fresh lime juice, 2 Tbsp. chopped fresh mint, 1 Tbsp. extra virgin olive oil, 1 tsp. kosher salt, and ½ tsp. freshly ground black pepper in a large bowl. Cover and chill 30 minutes to 1 hour. Thread 1 tomato piece, 1 watermelon cube, and 1 feta cube onto a 3-inch wooden skewer, and place in a serving bowl. Repeat with remaining skewers. Drizzle with remaining marinade, and serve immediately. (Makes about 36 skewers)

Tex-Mex Lasagna

No-cook lasagna noodles make prep for this Southwest-inspired lasagna a snap. Monterey Jack cheese gives a hint of spice, but if you crave more heat, swap out for hot habanero Jack cheese, instead.

2 large eggs, lightly beaten
1 (15-oz.) container ricotta
    cheese
1 (10-oz.) package frozen
    chopped spinach, thawed
    and well drained
¼ cup chopped fresh cilantro
½ tsp. table salt
4 cups (16 oz.) shredded
    Monterey Jack cheese with
    peppers, divided
2 (16-oz.) cans black beans,
    rinsed and drained
1 (2-lb., 13-oz.) jar pasta sauce
½ tsp. ground cumin
9 no-boil lasagna noodles

HANDS-ON: 20 MIN. ✦ **TOTAL:** 1 HR.

1. Preheat oven to 350°. Stir together first 5 ingredients and 1 cup Monterey Jack cheese; set aside.

2. Mash beans with a potato masher or fork in a large bowl; stir in pasta sauce and cumin. Spread one-third of bean mixture on bottom of a lightly greased 13- x 9-inch baking dish.

3. Top with 3 noodles, half of spinach mixture, and 1 cup Monterey Jack cheese. Repeat with 1 more layer spreading one-third bean mixture, remaining half of spinach mixture, and 1 cup Monterey Jack cheese, and 3 noodles; top with remaining bean mixture and remaining 3 noodles.

4. Bake, covered, at 350° for 1 hour; uncover and top with remaining 1 cup Monterey Jack cheese. Bake 5 more minutes or until cheese melts. (Serves 6 to 8)

Three-Cheese Pasta Bake

One cheese, two cheese, three cheese, yes please! This rich, cheesy bake is ideal as a meatless main, and it also pairs perfectly with grilled chicken or steak.

1 (16-oz.) package ziti, penne, or
  rigatoni
2 (10-oz.) containers refrigerated
  Alfredo sauce
1 (8-oz.) container sour cream
1 (15-oz.) container ricotta
  cheese
2 large eggs, lightly beaten
¼ cup grated Parmesan cheese
¼ cup chopped fresh parsley
1½ cups mozzarella cheese
Garnish: chopped fresh parsley

HANDS-ON: 20 MIN.　✦　**TOTAL:** 50 MIN.

1. Preheat oven to 350°. Cook pasta according to package directions; drain and return to pot.

2. Stir together Alfredo sauce and sour cream; toss with pasta until evenly coated. Spoon half of pasta mixture into a lightly greased 13- x 9 inch baking dish.

3. Stir together ricotta cheese and next 3 ingredients; spread evenly over pasta mixture in baking dish. Spoon remaining pasta mixture over ricotta cheese layer; sprinkle evenly with mozzarella cheese.

4. Bake at 350° for 30 minutes or until bubbly. (Serves 8 to 10)

NOTE: *We tested with Buitoni Refrigerated Alfredo Sauce.*

Green Bean Lasagna

This isn't your mom's green bean casserole. It's green bean lasagna, and it's much better. So much better even your mom will be impressed. We promise.

2 (14.4-oz.) packages frozen
   French-cut green beans,
   thawed
12 uncooked lasagna noodles
¼ cup butter, divided
2 large sweet onions, halved and
   sliced
8 oz. assorted fresh mushrooms,
   trimmed and sliced
¼ cup white wine
1 (15-oz.) container ricotta cheese
5 cups (20 oz.) shredded Italian
   cheese blend, divided
Parmesan Cream Sauce
1½ cups crushed round buttery
   crackers
1 (6-oz.) container French fried
   onions
3 Tbsp. butter, melted

HANDS-ON: 50 MIN. ✦ **TOTAL:** 2 HR., 25 MIN., INCLUDING SAUCE

1. Preheat oven to 350°. Drain green beans; pat dry with paper towels. Cook lasagna noodles according to package directions.

2. Meanwhile, melt 2 Tbsp. butter in a large skillet over medium-high heat; add onions, and sauté 15 minutes or until golden brown. Transfer onions to a large bowl, and wipe skillet clean.

3. Melt remaining 2 Tbsp. butter in skillet; add mushrooms, and sauté over medium-high heat 4 to 5 minutes or until tender. Add wine, and sauté 3 minutes or until liquid is absorbed. Add mushrooms and green beans to caramelized onions in bowl; toss.

4. Stir together ricotta cheese and 1 cup Italian cheese blend. Layer 1 cup Parmesan Cream Sauce, 3 noodles, half of green bean mixture, and 1 cup cheese blend in a lightly greased 15- x 10-inch baking dish. Top with 1 cup Parmesan Cream Sauce, 3 noodles, and all of ricotta cheese mixture. Top with 3 noodles, remaining green bean mixture, 1 cup cheese blend, and 1 cup Parmesan Cream Sauce. Top sauce with remaining 3 noodles, 1 cup Parmesan Cream Sauce, and 2 cups cheese blend.

5. Bake at 350° for 50 minutes or until bubbly and golden brown. Toss together crackers and next 2 ingredients. Remove lasagna from oven; sprinkle cracker mixture over top. Bake 10 more minutes. Let stand 20 minutes before serving. (Serves 8)

Parmesan Cream Sauce

HANDS-ON: 15 MIN. ✦ **TOTAL:** 15 MIN.

½ cup butter
⅓ cup all-purpose flour
4 cups milk

½ cup grated Parmesan cheese
¼ tsp. table salt
¼ tsp. freshly ground black pepper

Melt butter in a 3-qt. saucepan over medium-high heat. Whisk in flour; cook, whisking constantly, 1 minute. Gradually whisk in milk. Bring to a boil, and cook, whisking constantly, 1 to 2 minutes or until thickened. Whisk in Parmesan cheese, salt, and pepper. (Makes 4 cups)

Black Bean 'n' Spinach Enchiladas

These vegetarian enchiladas get a big flavor boost—and a little heat—from super simple Spinach Madeleine.

2 (15-oz.) cans black beans,
    rinsed and drained
2 Tbsp. fresh lime juice
1 tsp. Creole seasoning
1 tsp. chili powder
½ tsp. ground cumin
½ tsp. garlic powder
½ tsp. onion powder
½ recipe Spinach Madeleine
    (2 cups)
1 (8-oz.) container sour cream
8 (8-inch) flour tortillas
1 (12-oz.) block Monterey Jack
    cheese, shredded
Garnish: fresh parsley

HANDS-ON: 25 MIN. ✦ **TOTAL:** 1 HR., 10 MIN., INCLUDING SPINACH

1. Preheat oven to 350°. Combine first 7 ingredients in a medium bowl.

2. Stir together Spinach Madeleine and sour cream until blended.

3. Spoon about ½ cup black bean mixture down center of each tortilla. Top each with ⅓ cup Spinach Madeleine mixture, and sprinkle with 3 Tbsp. cheese. Roll up, and place, seam sides down, in 2 lightly greased 11- x 7-inch baking dishes. Sprinkle remaining cheese evenly over tops.

4. Bake, covered, at 350° for 25 minutes. Uncover and bake 5 to 10 more minutes or until cheese is melted. (Serves 8)

Spinach Madeleine

HANDS-ON: 25 MIN. ✦ **TOTAL:** 1 HR.

2 (10-oz.) packages frozen chopped spinach
¼ cup butter
½ tsp. minced fresh garlic
2 Tbsp. all-purpose flour
1 cup milk

1 (8-oz.) loaf pasteurized prepared cheese product,
    cubed
1 tsp. hot sauce
½ tsp. Creole seasoning

1. Cook spinach according to package directions; drain.

2. Meanwhile, melt butter in a medium saucepan over medium heat; add garlic, and sauté 1 minute. Whisk in flour until smooth, and cook, whisking constantly, 1 minute. Gradually whisk in milk, and cook, whisking constantly, 2 minutes or until mixture is thickened and bubbly.

3. Add cheese, hot sauce, and Creole seasoning; whisk until cheese is melted. Stir in spinach, and cook until thoroughly heated. Serve immediately. (Serves 8)

MASTER IT the FIRST TIME

BEANS

What's the difference between canned and dried? It's time to spill the beans.

COOKING DRIED BEANS

1. If you use dried beans in a recipe, soak them first to reduce the cooking time and help them get tender. There are two methods of soaking: quick soaking and overnight soaking.

2. Place the beans in a large Dutch oven, and add cool water to 2 inches above the beans. For a quick soak, bring the beans to a boil, and cook for 2 minutes. Remove the pan from the heat; cover and let stand 1 hour before draining. For an overnight soak, cover the Dutch oven, let stand for 8 hours or overnight, and then drain.

3. Place the drained soaked beans back in the large Dutch oven. Add water to 2 inches above the beans, and bring to a boil; make sure the beans stay covered with the liquid the entire time they are cooking.

4. Partially cover the pan, reduce the heat, and simmer until the beans are tender. Skim the foam from the surface of the cooking liquid as needed. It's important to cook the beans at a simmer, not a boil, since boiling can cook the beans too quickly and cause the skins to split.

5. Taste the beans to make sure they're tender. Don't just go by the estimated cooking times since older beans and those cooked in hard water will take longer to cook.

TIPS FOR TENDERNESS

- Soak the beans before cooking them in your recipe.

- Do not add ingredients such as lemon juice, vinegar, tomatoes, chili sauce, ketchup, molasses or wine until after the beans have been soaked and are fully cooked. Adding acidic ingredients or ingredients that are rich in calcium too early in the cooking process can prevent the beans from becoming tender.

- Add salt just before serving to avoid toughening bean skins.

mix it up

Get Canned: Canned beans are a convenient choice and can be substituted in recipes that call for dried, but keep in mind that the sodium is higher than dried. You can reduce the sodium by 40 percent by rinsing and draining the canned beans, but even then, you might want to decrease the amount of salt in the recipe. If you need to limit the sodium in your diet, look for no-salt-added canned beans or organic beans, which tend to be lower in sodium than regular canned beans.

Substituting canned beans for dried:
- 1 lb. dried beans (2 to 2½ cups) = 4½ to 5 cups cooked beans
- 1 cup dried beans = 2 to 2½ cups cooked beans
- 1 (15-oz.) can beans = 1¾ to 2 cups beans

Spanish-Style Lentils and Rice

Lentils may look small, but these mighty legumes are packed with protein and incredibly filling.

1 cup uncooked long-grain
    white rice
1 cup dried lentils
1 tsp. table salt
1 medium onion, diced
1 green bell pepper, diced
½ tsp. ground cumin
½ tsp. chili powder
¼ tsp. garlic powder
1 (10-oz.) can diced tomatoes
    with green chiles
1 cup (4 oz.) shredded sharp
    Cheddar cheese

HANDS-ON: 20 MIN.   ◆   **TOTAL:** 40 MIN.

1. Preheat oven to 350°. Bring 3½ cups water and first 3 ingredients to a boil in a medium saucepan; reduce heat, cover, and simmer 20 to 25 minutes or until lentils are tender.

2. Sauté onion and bell pepper in a large skillet over medium-high heat until tender. Add cumin, chili powder, and garlic powder; cook, stirring constantly, 2 minutes.

3. Stir onion mixture and tomatoes into rice mixture, and spoon into a lightly greased 13- x 9-inch baking dish.

4. Bake at 350° for 15 minutes; top evenly with shredded Cheddar cheese, and bake 5 more minutes. (Serves 6)

serve it on the side

Caesar Salad Bites: Separate 2 romaine lettuce hearts into 24 medium leaves, and arrange on a large platter. Evenly divide ⅔ cup bottled refrigerated creamy Caesar dressing down center of each leaf. Top with ½ chopped English cucumber, 1¼ cups small seasoned croutons, 1 cup sliced grape tomatoes and ¼ cup coarsely chopped fresh parsley. Sprinkle with freshly ground black pepper to taste. (Serves 6 to 8)

Cheesy Broccoli-and-Rice Casserole *(pictured on page 128)*

Major makeover alert: Cremini mushrooms, panko, and fresh broccoli elevate this classic dish to the next level.

6 Tbsp. unsalted butter, divided

1 cup panko (Japanese breadcrumbs)

2 cups (8 oz.) shredded extra-sharp Cheddar cheese, divided

3 cups chicken broth

2 cups milk

1 bay leaf

1 fresh thyme sprig

2 cups chopped onion

½ cup diced celery

1 (8-oz.) package sliced cremini mushrooms

1 tsp. kosher salt, divided

Pinch of freshly ground black pepper

Pinch of ground red pepper

2 garlic cloves, minced

¼ cup all-purpose flour

1½ cups uncooked long-grain rice

½ cup sour cream

½ cup mayonnaise

⅛ tsp. freshly grated nutmeg

3 cups fresh broccoli

HANDS-ON: 30 MIN.   ✦   **TOTAL:** 1 HR., 5 MIN.

1. Preheat oven to 350°. Melt 2 Tbsp. butter. Combine melted butter with panko and 1 cup shredded Cheddar cheese; toss to coat.

2. Bring broth and next 3 ingredients to a simmer in a medium saucepan over medium-low heat. Reduce heat to low; cover and keep warm until ready to use.

3. Melt remaining 4 Tbsp. butter in a large shallow Dutch oven or ovenproof skillet over medium heat. Add onion and celery, and cook, stirring occasionally, 3 to 5 minutes or until onion is lightly browned. Add mushrooms and ½ tsp. kosher salt and a pinch each of black pepper and ground red pepper. Cook, stirring occasionally, 3 to 5 minutes or until mushrooms are tender. Add garlic, and cook, stirring constantly, 45 seconds. Stir in flour until combined. (Mixture will be dry.)

4. Remove and discard bay leaf and thyme from broth mixture. Gradually stir warm broth mixture into mushroom mixture. Add remaining 1 cup cheese, and stir until well blended and smooth. Stir in rice and next 3 ingredients.

5. Bake, covered, at 350° for 25 to 30 minutes or until rice is tender and liquid is absorbed. Remove from oven; increase oven temperature to broil.

6. Microwave broccoli, ¼ cup water, and remaining ½ tsp. kosher salt in a covered microwave-safe bowl at HIGH about 2 minutes or just until broccoli is tender and bright green. Drain and pat broccoli dry. Stir broccoli into rice mixture.

7. Sprinkle breadcrumb mixture over broccoli mixture. Place on middle oven rack, and broil 2 to 3 minutes or until topping is golden brown. Let stand 5 minutes before serving. (Serves 8 to 10)

Sweet Potato, Cauliflower, and Greens Casserole

Big on vitamins and flavor, this hearty main course will fill you up without weighing you down.

1 head cauliflower (1½ to 2 lb.), cut into small florets

1 (8-oz.) package fresh cremini mushrooms, stemmed and halved

6 Tbsp. olive oil, divided

1 tsp. ground cumin, divided

1 tsp. kosher salt, divided

¼ tsp. freshly ground black pepper, divided

3 large sweet potatoes, peeled and cut into ¼-inch-thick slices

2 garlic cloves, minced

4 cups chopped fresh kale, collards, or mustard greens

2 tsp. red wine vinegar

1 (14-oz.) can butter beans, drained and rinsed (optional)

1½ cups Easy Cheese Sauce (page 16)

½ cup panko (Japanese breadcrumbs)

1 Tbsp. chopped cilantro

1 tsp. extra virgin olive oil

HANDS-ON: 55 MIN.　✦　**TOTAL:** 1 HR., 45 MIN.

1. Preheat oven to 475°. Toss together cauliflower, mushrooms, 2½ Tbsp. oil, ½ tsp. cumin, ½ tsp. salt, and ⅛ tsp. pepper in a medium bowl. Spread cauliflower mixture in a single layer in jelly-roll pan.

2. Toss together sweet potatoes, 2½ Tbsp. oil, and remaining cumin, salt, and pepper. Spread in a single layer in another jelly-roll pan.

3. Bake potatoes and cauliflower mixture at 475° for 10 to 12 minutes or until browned and just tender, turning once. Cool 10 minutes.

4. Reduce oven temperature to 375°. Heat remaining 1 Tbsp. oil in a large skillet over medium-high heat. Add garlic; cook, stirring often, 1 minute. Add kale; cook, stirring occasionally, 10 minutes or until tender. Add salt and pepper to taste; stir in vinegar.

5. Layer half each of sweet potatoes, cauliflower mixture, butter beans, if desired, kale, and ½ cup Easy Cheese Sauce in a lightly greased 13- x 9-inch baking dish. Repeat layers once. Top with remaining ½ cup cheese sauce. Stir together panko, chopped cilantro, and 1 tsp. olive oil, and sprinkle crumb mixture over casserole.

6. Bake at 375° for 20 to 25 minutes or until thoroughly heated and golden brown. Let stand 5 minutes before serving. (Serves 6 to 8)

Gnocchi á la Narciso

Get a jump start on next week's dinner by freezing some extra uncooked gnocchi on a baking sheet; store it in heavy-duty zip-top plastic bags for up to 2 months. When you're ready to cook it, just boil as directed for 5 to 6 minutes.

3 large russet potatoes
Vegetable oil
2 cups all-purpose flour
2 large eggs
⅓ cup butter, melted
½ tsp. table salt
¾ tsp. freshly ground black pepper
4 cups Basic Marinara (page 16)
3 cups grated Parmesan or Asiago cheese

HANDS-ON: 45 MIN. ✦ **TOTAL:** 1 HR., 10 MIN.

1. Preheat oven to 400°. Scrub potatoes, and pat dry. Rub with oil, and wrap in aluminum foil.

2. Bake at 400° for 1 hour or until tender. Remove from oven, and reduce oven temperature to 350°. Peel potatoes, discarding skins; mash pulp with a fork.

3. Beat potato pulp, 2 cups flour, and next 4 ingredients at medium speed with an electric mixer until blended.

4. Turn dough out onto a well-floured surface. Divide dough into 8 equal portions, and coat each portion with flour. Knead portions with well-floured hands until smooth and elastic and no longer sticky. Roll each portion into ¾-inch diameter ropes; cut each rope into ¾-inch lengths. Place dough pieces on floured baking sheets.

5. Bring 3 qt. water to a boil over medium-high heat in a large Dutch oven. Drop gnocchi, 10 to 12 at a time, into water, and cook 3 to 4 minutes or until gnocchi rises to the top.

6. Spread 1 cup Basic Marinara in bottom of a lightly greased 13- x 9-inch baking dish; top with one-fourth of gnocchi, and sprinkle with ¾ cup Parmesan cheese. Repeat layers 3 times with sauce, remaining gnocchi, and cheese.

7. Bake at 350° for 20 to 30 minutes. (Serves 12 to 14)

Savory Vegetable Bread Pudding

Not all bread puddings have to be sweet. This savory option is filled with sautéed fresh veggies, garlic, and cheese, and it makes a great option for the holidays.

1 bunch Swiss chard

6 large eggs

1 cup milk

2 tsp. Dijon mustard

1¼ tsp. table salt

¾ tsp. freshly ground black
   pepper

3 cups cubed ciabatta bread

1½ cups freshly grated Parmesan
   cheese, divided

1 (8-oz.) package sliced fresh
   mushrooms

1 red bell pepper, chopped

1 small onion, chopped

1 tsp. minced garlic

2 Tbsp. olive oil

HANDS-ON: 20 MIN. ✦ **TOTAL:** 1 HR., 10 MIN.

1. Preheat oven to 350°. Remove and discard ribs from Swiss chard. Rinse with cold water; drain and coarsely chop.

2. Whisk together eggs and next 4 ingredients in a large bowl; stir in bread and ¾ cup cheese.

3. Sauté mushrooms and next 3 ingredients in hot oil in a large skillet over medium-high heat 8 minutes. Stir in Swiss chard, and sauté 2 minutes. Fold vegetable mixture into egg mixture. Pour into a lightly greased 11- x 7-inch baking dish. Sprinkle with remaining ¾ cup cheese.

4. Bake at 350° for 35 to 40 minutes or until center is set. Let stand 5 minutes. (Serves 4 to 6)

mix it up

Okra-Tomato Bread Pudding: Omit mushrooms and Swiss chard. Substitute shredded Monterey Jack cheese for Parmesan cheese, 1½ tsp. Cajun seasoning for table salt, and green bell pepper for red bell pepper. Reduce black pepper to ½ tsp.

Prepare recipe as directed in Step 2, adding 2 Tbsp. chopped fresh flat-leaf parsley, and 2 medium tomatoes, chopped, with bread. Proceed with recipe as directed, sautéing 2 cups sliced okra with onion 8 to 10 minutes in Step 3. (Serves 4 to 6)

Portobello 'n' Shiitake Mushroom Pot Pies

For the best flavor, choose plump shiitakes with edges that curl under, and avoid those with broken caps.

1 (12-oz.) French bread baguette
3 Tbsp. butter
1 large sweet onion, sliced
¼ lb. shiitake mushrooms, sliced
½ lb. portobello mushrooms, sliced
2 garlic cloves, pressed
1 (14.5-oz.) can vegetable broth
¼ cup dry red wine or vegetable broth
2 Tbsp. all-purpose flour
¼ tsp. freshly ground black pepper
¼ cup (1 oz.) shredded Italian cheese blend
2 Tbsp. chopped fresh parsley
Garnish: fried sage leaves

HANDS-ON: 30 MIN. ✦ **TOTAL:** 1 HR.

1. Preheat oven to 400°. Cut baguette into 4 (1-inch-thick) slices and 8 (¼-inch-thick) slices, and place on a baking sheet. Reserve remaining baguette for another use.

2. Bake at 400° for 5 minutes or until toasted. Remove bread slices from oven; reduce oven temperature to 350°.

3. Melt butter in a large skillet over medium heat; add onion, and cook, stirring often, 20 minutes or until caramel colored. Add mushrooms and garlic, and cook, stirring constantly, 3 minutes. Stir in broth and wine; bring to a boil. Reduce heat, and simmer, stirring occasionally, 20 minutes or until slightly thickened.

4. Stir together ½ cup water and flour until smooth. Stir flour mixture and pepper into mushroom mixture; cook, stirring constantly, 1 minute.

5. Place 1-inch-thick baguette slices in bottoms of 4 (8-oz.) ramekins or ovenproof glass bowls. Spoon mushroom mixture evenly over bread slices in ramekins. Top each with 2 (¼-inch-thick) baguette slices. Sprinkle with cheese.

6. Bake at 350° for 5 minutes or until cheese melts. Sprinkle with parsley. (Serves 4)

dress it up

Fried sage leaves make a gorgeous garnish. Rinse 20 large fresh sage leaves and lay flat on a double layer of paper towels; cover with more towels and press gently to flatten and dry leaves. Pour olive or canola oil into a shallow 1 to 1½-qt. saucepan over medium-high heat to a depth of ¼ inch. When hot (oil will ripple), lower heat to medium and add sage leaves, a few at a time, in a single layer. Fry until oil stops bubbling around leaves, 10 to 15 seconds (do not let brown), then remove carefully with tongs and drain on more paper towels. Sprinkle with table salt to taste. Use immediately, or store between layers of paper towels in an airtight container at room temperature up to 1 day.

Vegetable Pot Pie with Parmesan-Black Pepper Biscuits

Meatless Monday was made with this recipe in mind: an easy combination of fresh and frozen veggies.

FILLING

2 cups diced peeled baking
    potato
1¼ cups diced carrot
1 cup diced parsnip
¾ cup chopped celery
2 (8-oz.) packages presliced
    cremini mushrooms
¼ tsp. table salt
½ tsp. freshly ground black
    pepper
2 Tbsp. olive oil, divided
2 garlic cloves, minced
Vegetable cooking spray
2½ Tbsp. all-purpose flour
1½ cups milk
¾ cup organic vegetable broth
2 cups frozen petite green peas
1½ Tbsp. chopped fresh thyme
1 (16-oz.) package frozen pearl
    onions

BISCUIT TOPPING

1⅔ cups all-purpose flour
1½ tsp. baking powder
¾ tsp. baking soda
⅛ tsp. table salt
1 tsp. freshly ground black
    pepper
4½ Tbsp. unsalted butter, cut
    into pieces
2 oz. grated fresh Parmesan
    cheese
3 Tbsp. chopped fresh chives
1 cup buttermilk

HANDS-ON: 30 MIN. ✦ **TOTAL:** 5 HR., 20 MIN.

1. **Prepare Filling:** Sauté potato and next 6 ingredients in ½ Tbsp. hot oil in large nonstick skillet over medium-high heat for 5 minutes. Add garlic; sauté 1 minute. Coat a 5-qt. electric slow cooker with cooking spray. Transfer vegetable mixture to slow cooker.

2. Heat remaining 1½ Tbsp. olive oil in skillet over medium-high heat. Add 2½ Tbsp. flour; cook 1 minute, stirring until smooth. Whisk in milk and broth; cook over medium heat 3 minutes, stirring constantly, or until thickened and bubbly. Pour sauce into slow cooker. Stir in peas, thyme, and onions. Cover and cook on LOW for 3½ hours or until vegetables are tender.

3. **Prepare Biscuit Topping:** Combine flour, baking powder, and next 3 ingredients in a large bowl. Cut in butter with a pastry blender or fork until mixture resembles small peas. Stir in cheese and chives. Add buttermilk, stirring just until dry ingredients are moistened.

4. Increase slow cooker heat to HIGH. Drop large spoonfuls of Biscuit Topping onto filling in 8 equal mounds. Cover and cook on HIGH for 1 hour and 15 minutes or until biscuits are done. Uncover and let stand 5 minutes before serving. (Serves 8)

serve it on the side

Spicy Roasted Red Bell Pepper Pimiento Cheese: Stir together 1¼ cups mayonnaise; ½ (12-oz.) jar roasted red bell peppers, drained and chopped; 2 tsp. finely grated onion; 2 tsp. coarse-grained mustard; and ½ tsp. ground red pepper. Stir in 2 (10-oz.) blocks sharp white Cheddar cheese, shredded, and freshly ground black pepper to taste. Serve immediately, or store in an airtight container in refrigerator up to 4 days. (Makes 4 cups)

Spring Onion Pie

The workhorse of so many dishes, onions step into the spotlight in this easy recipe. The accompanying Gruyère cheese adds a sweet but slightly salty flavor, without overshadowing the onion.

10 thin spring onions

4 large eggs, lightly beaten

1 cup milk

¾ cup all-purpose flour

1 tsp. kosher salt

½ tsp. baking powder

¼ tsp. freshly ground black pepper

2 Tbsp. butter

5 oz. Gruyère cheese, cubed

HANDS-ON: 20 MIN. ✦ **TOTAL:** 45 MIN.

1. Preheat oven to 400°. Heat a 10-inch cast-iron skillet in oven. Trim roots from onions; discard roots. Chop half of onions.

2. Whisk together eggs and milk. Sift together flour and next 3 ingredients. Gradually add flour mixture to egg mixture, whisking rapidly 20 to 30 seconds or just until blended and smooth. (There should be no lumps.) Stir in chopped onions. Let stand 5 minutes.

3. Carefully remove hot skillet from oven. Add butter, and let stand until butter is melted. Place skillet over medium-high heat, and pour batter into skillet. Arrange cheese and remaining whole onions over top of batter, and cook 30 seconds to 1 minute or until edges begin to set.

4. Transfer skillet to top oven rack, and bake at 400° for 22 to 25 minutes or until golden brown and puffy. (Outside edges should be crispy, and inside texture should resemble a custard popover. Pie will deflate quickly.) Serve immediately. (Serves 6)

Squash Frittata

This quick-and-easy frittata will be one of your go-to favorites after a long day of work and busy school activities. It's simple to throw together and swap out ingredients according to what's in your fridge.

6 large eggs, lightly beaten

2 Tbsp. heavy cream

½ tsp. kosher salt, divided

¼ lb. fingerling potatoes, cut into ¼-inch-thick slices

2 Tbsp. canola oil

1 Tbsp. butter

2 small zucchini, cut into ¼-inch-thick slices (about 1 cup)

2 small yellow squash, cut into ¼-inch-thick slices (about 1 cup)

4 Tbsp. freshly grated Parmesan cheese

Garnish: fresh basil leaves

HANDS-ON: 25 MIN. ✦ **TOTAL:** 35 MIN.

1. Preheat oven to 350°. Whisk together eggs, cream, and ¼ tsp. salt.

2. Cook potatoes in hot oil in a 10-inch ovenproof nonstick skillet over medium-high heat, stirring often, 1 minute. Sprinkle with remaining ¼ tsp salt. Reduce heat to medium, and cook, stirring often, 3 to 4 minutes or until light golden brown on both sides. Transfer potatoes to a bowl.

3. Return skillet to heat; melt 1 tsp. butter in skillet. Add zucchini and yellow squash; cook, stirring often, 2 to 3 minutes or until crisp-tender. Add remaining 2 tsp. butter to skillet; let melt. Add potatoes, stirring to coat.

4. Pour egg mixture over potatoes. Reduce heat to medium-low; cook 1 minute. Sprinkle with cheese.

5. Bake at 350° for 8 to 9 minutes or until center is set. Remove from oven. (Serves 6 to 8)

Sweet Onion
Casserole, page 179

chapter 4

toss-together sides

Don't tell the other courses, but sides have more personality than any other part of the meal. Chicken, steak, and fish may get to sit in the center of the table, but it's the Pimiento Cheese Creamed Spinach, Caramelized Onion Mashed Potato Bake, and Green Bean-Goat Cheese Gratin that add big helpings of wow to each plate.

Savory Tomato Cobbler

The stone-ground cornmeal in the recipe adds texture to the biscuit-like crust, but you can use plain cornmeal or your favorite biscuit recipe, instead.

1 medium-size sweet onion, chopped

1 Tbsp. olive oil

1 large tomato, chopped

3 garlic cloves, minced

3 lb. assorted small tomatoes, divided

1 Tbsp. Champagne vinegar or white wine vinegar

1 Tbsp. cornstarch

1 tsp. kosher salt

1 tsp. freshly ground black pepper

1 tsp. fresh thyme leaves

1½ cups self-rising soft-wheat flour (such as White Lily)

½ cup stone-ground yellow cornmeal

½ tsp. baking powder

½ cup cold butter, cut into ¼-inch-thick pieces

¾ cup (6 oz.) freshly shredded Jarlsberg cheese

¼ cup chopped fresh basil

2 Tbsp. chopped fresh chives

1¼ cups buttermilk

HANDS-ON: 45 MIN. ✦ **TOTAL:** 1 HR., 55 MIN.

1. Preheat oven to 375°. Sauté onion in hot oil in a large skillet over medium-high heat 5 to 6 minutes or until tender. Add chopped tomato, garlic, and 1½ cups small tomatoes, and sauté 10 minutes or until tomatoes are softened. Remove from heat, and stir in vinegar and next 4 ingredients.

2. Place remaining tomatoes in a 13- x 9-inch baking dish. Spoon onion mixture over tomatoes, and gently toss to coat. Bake at 375° for 10 minutes.

3. Meanwhile, stir together flour and next 2 ingredients in a large bowl. Cut butter into flour with a pastry blender until mixture resembles small peas; cover and chill 10 minutes. Stir cheese and next 2 ingredients into cold flour mixture. Add buttermilk, stirring just until dry ingredients are moistened. Dollop mixture by ½ cupfuls onto tomato mixture. (Do not spread.)

4. Bake at 375° for 30 to 35 minutes or until golden brown. Cool on a wire rack 30 minutes before serving. (Serves 6 to 8)

Zucchini-Potato Casserole

The beauty of this casserole is in the layering. The stacked potatoes, tomatoes, and zucchini are in the style of a tian, *a French dish of layered vegetables, giving the dish an elegant presentation unlike most casseroles you're used to. Don't be afraid to play with colors—try a variety of heirloom tomatoes, yellow squash, and even purple potatoes!*

2 Tbsp. butter

2 medium-size sweet onions, chopped

Vegetable cooking spray

1 medium Yukon gold potato, sliced

1 medium zucchini, sliced

4 plum tomatoes, sliced

1½ tsp. kosher salt

¾ tsp. freshly ground black pepper

2 Tbsp. butter, melted

⅓ cup freshly grated Parmesan cheese

HANDS-ON: 35 MIN.   ✦   **TOTAL:** 1 HR., 50 MIN.

1. Preheat oven to 375°. Melt 2 Tbsp. butter in a medium skillet over medium heat; add onions, and sauté 10 to 12 minutes or until tender and onions begin to caramelize.

2. Spoon onions into a 10-inch pie plate coated with cooking spray. Toss together potatoes and next 4 ingredients. Arrange potatoes, zucchini, and tomatoes in a single layer over onions, alternating and overlapping slightly. Drizzle with 2 Tbsp. melted butter. Cover with aluminum foil.

3. Bake at 375° for 30 minutes. Remove foil, and sprinkle with cheese. Bake 35 to 40 more minutes or until golden brown. Let stand 10 minutes before serving. (Serves 6 to 8)

Summer Squash Casserole

Summer squash is mild in flavor with thin, edible skin. It's also high in water content and doesn't require long cooking times, which makes it ideal for all sorts of casseroles. Just be sure to drain cooked squash well before mixing it with other ingredients so your casserole doesn't end up too soupy.

1½ lb. yellow squash

1 lb. zucchini

1 small sweet onion, chopped

2½ tsp. table salt, divided

1 cup grated carrots

1 (10 ¾-oz.) can cream of chicken soup

1 (8-oz.) container sour cream

1 (8-oz.) can water chestnuts, drained and chopped

1 (8-oz.) package herb-seasoned stuffing

½ cup butter, melted

HANDS-ON: 25 MIN. ✦ **TOTAL:** 50 MIN.

1. Preheat oven to 350°. Cut squash and zucchini into ¼-inch-thick slices; place in a Dutch oven. Add chopped onion, 2 tsp. salt, and water to cover. Bring to a boil over medium-high heat, and cook 5 minutes; drain well.

2. Stir together 1 cup grated carrots, next 3 ingredients, and remaining ½ tsp. salt in a large bowl; fold in squash mixture. Stir together stuffing and ½ cup melted butter, and spoon half of stuffing mixture into bottom of a lightly greased 13- x 9-inch baking dish. Spoon squash mixture over stuffing mixture, and top with remaining stuffing mixture.

3. Bake at 350° for 30 to 35 minutes or until bubbly and golden brown, shielding with aluminum foil after 20 to 25 minutes to prevent excessive browning, if necessary. Let stand 10 minutes before serving. (Serves 8)

NOTE: *We tested with Pepperidge Farm Herb Seasoned Stuffing.*

Sweet Potato-Carrot Casserole

Adding cooked carrots to this comfort food classic creates a smooth texture and enhances the sweet flavor.
Top it with marshmallows and spicy-sweet pecans for an even sugarier crunch.

6 large sweet potatoes (about 5 lb.)
1½ lb. carrots, sliced
¼ cup butter
1 cup sour cream
2 Tbsp. sugar
1 tsp. firmly packed lemon zest
½ tsp. table salt
½ tsp. ground nutmeg
½ tsp. freshly ground black pepper
1½ cups miniature marshmallows
1 cup Sugar-and-Spice Pecans

HANDS-ON: 40 MIN. ✦ **TOTAL:** 3 HR., 40 MIN., INCLUDING PECANS

1. Preheat oven to 400°. Bake sweet potatoes on a baking sheet 1 hour or until tender. Reduce oven temperature to 350°. Let potatoes stand until cool to touch (about 20 minutes).

2. Meanwhile, cook carrots in boiling water to cover 20 to 25 minutes or until very tender; drain.

3. Process carrots and butter in a food processor until smooth, stopping to scrape down sides as needed. Transfer carrot mixture to a large bowl.

4. Peel and cube sweet potatoes. Process, in batches, in food processor until smooth, stopping to scrape down sides as needed. Add sweet potatoes to carrot mixture. Stir in sour cream and next 5 ingredients, stirring until blended. Spoon mixture into a lightly greased 13- x 9-inch baking dish.

5. Bake at 350° for 30 minutes or until thoroughly heated. Remove from oven. Sprinkle with marshmallows. Bake 10 more minutes or until marshmallows are golden brown. Remove from oven, and sprinkle with Sugar-and-Spice Pecans. (Serves 8 to 10)

Sugar-and-Spice Pecans

HANDS-ON: 15 MIN. ✦ **TOTAL:** 1 HR., 10 MIN.

1 egg white
4 cups pecan halves and pieces
½ cup sugar

1 Tbsp. orange zest
1 tsp. ground cinnamon
1 tsp. ground ginger

1. Preheat oven to 350°. Whisk egg white in a large bowl until foamy. Add pecans, and stir until evenly coated.

2. Stir together sugar and next 3 ingredients in a small bowl until blended. Sprinkle sugar mixture over pecans; stir gently until pecans are evenly coated. Spread pecans in a single layer in a lightly greased aluminum foil-lined 15- x 10-inch jelly-roll pan.

3. Bake at 350° for 24 to 26 minutes or until pecans are toasted and dry, stirring once after 10 minutes. Remove from oven, and cool completely (about 30 minutes). (Makes 4 cups)

Green Bean-Goat Cheese Gratin

Breadcrumbs and toasted pecans tossed with Parmesan and olive oil are sprinkled over these individual gratins, giving them the crunch factor we all crave when it comes to the green bean casserole.

2 white bread slices
1 Tbsp. olive oil
¾ cup (3 oz.) freshly shredded
    Parmesan cheese, divided
⅓ cup finely chopped pecans
1 lb. fresh haricots verts (French
    green beans), trimmed
2 oz. goat cheese, crumbled
½ cup whipping cream
¼ tsp. kosher salt
¼ tsp. freshly ground black
    pepper

HANDS-ON: 20 MIN. ✦ **TOTAL:** 50 MIN.

1. Preheat oven to 400°. Tear bread into large pieces; pulse in a food processor 2 or 3 times or until coarse crumbs form. Drizzle oil over crumbs; add ¼ cup Parmesan cheese. Pulse 5 or 6 times or until coated with oil. Stir in pecans.

2. Cut green beans crosswise into thirds. Cook in boiling water to cover 3 to 4 minutes or until crisp-tender; drain. Plunge into ice water to stop the cooking process; drain and pat dry with paper towels.

3. Toss together beans, next 4 ingredients, and remaining ½ cup Parmesan cheese. Firmly pack mixture into 4 (6-oz.) shallow ramekins. Cover each with aluminum foil, and place on a baking sheet.

4. Bake at 400° for 20 minutes. Uncover and sprinkle with crumb mixture. Bake 8 more minutes or until golden. Let stand 5 minutes. (Serves 4)

dress it up

Lemon zest looks and tastes great, and adds a burst of fresh flavor to green bean gratin. Wash and dry 1 lemon. Grate it with a grater or lemon zester, being careful not to grate the white pith. If you don't use all the zest, freeze it for future dishes.

Home-style Green Bean Casserole

It's not the holidays without green bean casserole, but this version is a more modern take on the traditional you know. The addition of mushrooms, tomatoes, and panko takes it from ordinary to extraordinary.

1½ lb. fresh green beans, trimmed

2 Tbsp. butter

¼ cup all-purpose flour

1½ cups 2% reduced-fat milk

½ cup nonfat buttermilk

1 Tbsp. Ranch dressing mix

2 tsp. chopped fresh thyme

¼ tsp. table salt

¼ tsp. freshly ground black pepper

1 tsp. butter

1 (8-oz.) package sliced fresh mushrooms

Vegetable cooking spray

1 cup French fried onions, crushed

½ cup panko (Japanese breadcrumbs)

2 plum tomatoes, seeded and chopped

HANDS-ON: 25 MIN. ✦ **TOTAL:** 55 MIN.

1. Preheat oven to 350°. Cook green beans in boiling salted water to cover in a Dutch oven 4 to 6 minutes or to desired degree of doneness; drain. Plunge into ice water to stop the cooking process; drain and pat dry.

2. Melt 2 Tbsp. butter in Dutch oven over medium heat; whisk in flour until smooth. Cook, whisking constantly, 1 minute. Gradually whisk in 1½ cups milk; cook, whisking constantly, 3 to 4 minutes or until sauce is thickened and bubbly. Remove from heat, and whisk in buttermilk and next 4 ingredients.

3. Melt 1 tsp. butter in a medium skillet over medium-high heat; add mushrooms, and sauté 6 to 8 minutes or until lightly browned. Remove from heat; let stand 5 minutes. Gently toss mushrooms and green beans in buttermilk sauce. Place in a 13- x 9-inch or 3-qt. baking dish coated with cooking spray.

4. Combine French fried onions and next 2 ingredients; sprinkle over green bean mixture.

5. Bake at 350° for 25 to 30 minutes or until golden brown and bubbly. Serve immediately. (Serves 8)

Cauliflower Gratin with Almond Crust

A little Gruyère and cream turns the common cauliflower into a superstar side. Choose a firm head of cauliflower with compact florets, and crisp green leaves. Add some flair to the gratin by mixing in green or purple cauliflower florets, in addition to white (the purple turn pale green when cooked).

¼ cup butter

1 head cauliflower (about 2¼ lb.), separated into florets

1 small onion, chopped

2 garlic cloves, minced

2 Tbsp. all-purpose flour

2 tsp. chopped fresh thyme

½ tsp. table salt

½ cup whipping cream

1 cup (4 oz.) shredded Gruyère cheese

⅔ cup panko (Japanese breadcrumbs)

¼ cup sliced almonds

¼ cup grated Parmesan cheese

HANDS-ON: 25 MIN. ✦ **TOTAL:** 45 MIN.

1. Preheat oven to 400°. Melt butter in a large skillet over medium-high heat. Add cauliflower and next 2 ingredients; sauté 10 minutes or until golden and just tender. Sprinkle with flour and next 2 ingredients; stir well. Remove from heat.

2. Spoon cauliflower mixture into an 11- x 7-inch baking dish, and drizzle with cream. Sprinkle with Gruyère cheese and next 3 ingredients.

3. Bake at 400° for 18 to 20 minutes or until golden. (Serves 6)

mix it up

Cauliflower and Broccoli Gratin with Almond Crust: Substitute ½ head cauliflower and ½ head broccoli (about 2¼ lb., separated into florets) for the 1 head cauliflower. Prepare recipe as directed.

Zucchini, Squash, and Corn Casserole

Pulse day-old sandwich bread in the food processor to create fresh breadcrumbs. They'll do double duty in this dish as a binder and topping.

1½ lb. yellow squash, cut into ¼-inch-thick slices

1½ lb. zucchini, cut into ¼-inch-thick slices

¼ cup butter, divided

2 cups diced sweet onion

2 garlic cloves, minced

3 cups fresh corn kernels

1½ cups (6 oz.) freshly shredded white Cheddar cheese

½ cup sour cream

½ cup mayonnaise

2 large eggs, lightly beaten

2 tsp. freshly ground black pepper

1 tsp. table salt

1½ cups soft, fresh breadcrumbs, divided

1 cup freshly grated Asiago cheese, divided

HANDS-ON: 15 MIN. ✦ **TOTAL:** 1 HR., 20 MIN.

1. Preheat oven to 350°. Bring first 2 ingredients and water to cover to a boil in a Dutch oven over medium-high heat, and boil 5 minutes or until crisp-tender. Drain; gently press between paper towels.

2. Melt 2 Tbsp. butter in a skillet over medium-high heat; add onion, and sauté 10 minutes or until tender. Add garlic, and sauté 2 minutes.

3. Stir together squash, onion mixture, corn, next 6 ingredients, and ½ cup each breadcrumbs and Asiago cheese just until blended. Spoon mixture into a lightly greased 13- x 9-inch baking dish.

4. Melt remaining 2 Tbsp. butter. Stir in remaining 1 cup breadcrumbs and ½ cup Asiago cheese. Sprinkle over casserole.

5. Bake at 350° for 45 to 50 minutes or until golden brown and set. Let stand 15 minutes before serving. (Serves 8 to 10)

Sweet Corn Pudding

Fresh corn is the star of this easy side. Use a corn cutter and creamer to make easy work of removing the corn kernels and extracting the sweet juices. You can also use a chef's knife by scraping the cob with the side of the knife—just be sure you're getting all of the milk.

9 ears fresh corn, husks removed
4 large eggs, beaten
½ cup half-and-half
1½ tsp. baking powder
⅓ cup butter
2 Tbsp. sugar
2 Tbsp. all-purpose flour
1 Tbsp. butter, melted
⅛ tsp. freshly ground black pepper
Garnish: chopped fresh chives

HANDS-ON: 30 MIN.   ✦   **TOTAL:** 1 HR., 17 MIN.

1. Preheat oven to 350°. Cut off tips of corn kernels into a bowl; scrape milk and remaining pulp from cob with a paring knife to measure 3 to 4 cups.

2. Combine eggs, half-and-half, and baking powder, stirring well with a wire whisk.

3. Melt ⅓ cup butter in a large saucepan over low heat; add sugar and flour, stirring until smooth. Remove from heat; gradually add egg mixture, whisking constantly until smooth. Stir in corn. Pour corn mixture into a greased 1- or 1½-qt. baking dish.

4. Bake at 350° for 40 to 45 minutes or until pudding is set. Drizzle with 1 Tbsp. melted butter; sprinkle with pepper.

5. Increase heat to broil. Broil pudding 5½ inches from heat 2 minutes or until golden. Let stand 5 minutes before serving. (Serves 6 to 8)

Wild Rice-and-Greens Casserole

All hail kale, the superhero green with health benefits galore. It's hearty enough to stand up to sun-dried tomatoes and Gruyère without overpowering the dish. Choose bright and rich-colored kale, in small bunches, and don't store it in the refrigerator for more than two to three days. Any longer than that and the flavor can become too strong.

½ lb. fresh kale or other hearty
    greens, trimmed and
    coarsely chopped
1 medium onion, chopped
4½ tsp. olive oil
3 garlic cloves, minced
1 Tbsp. fresh thyme leaves
¼ tsp. ground nutmeg
4 Tbsp. all-purpose flour
1 cup milk
1 cup chicken broth
3 cups cooked wild rice
½ cup chopped sun-dried
    tomatoes
1 cup grated Gruyère cheese,
    divided*
Vegetable cooking spray
½ cup chopped almonds

HANDS-ON: 50 MIN. ✦ **TOTAL:** 1 HR., 10 MIN.

1. Preheat oven to 375°. Cook kale in 1 cup boiling salted water in a Dutch oven over high heat, stirring occasionally, 5 minutes; drain.

2. Cook onion in hot oil in a large skillet over medium-low heat, stirring often, 20 minutes or until golden. Add garlic, thyme, and nutmeg, and cook 1 minute. Stir in flour and cooked kale. Gradually stir in milk and broth, and cook, stirring often, 4 minutes or until thickened. Stir in rice, tomatoes, and ½ cup cheese. Add table salt and freshly ground black pepper to taste.

3. Transfer mixture to a 2½-qt. baking dish coated with cooking spray. Sprinkle almonds and remaining ½ cup cheese over mixture.

4. Bake at 375° for 18 minutes or until bubbly and lightly browned. (Serves 8)

* Swiss cheese may be substituted.

Hoppin' John Bake

Hoppin' John is a Southern New Year's traditional dish said to bring good luck. But this mix of black-eyed peas, rice, and bell pepper is definitely too good for just one annual appearance. Our twist adds cheese and bakes it for extra goodness.

½ (16-oz.) package dried black-eyed peas

4 cups chicken broth, plus additional for rice

1 cup uncooked long-grain rice

3 center-cut bacon slices

1 red bell pepper, finely chopped

1 yellow onion, finely chopped

2 garlic cloves, minced

½ tsp. table salt

¼ tsp. freshly ground black pepper

8 oz. Monterey Jack cheese

Garnish: chopped fresh flat-leaf parsley

HANDS-ON: 45 MIN. ✦ **TOTAL:** 9 HR., 50 MIN., INCLUDING SOAKING TIME

1. Rinse and sort peas according to package directions. Cover with water 3 inches above peas; let soak 8 hours. Drain and rinse well.

2. Combine peas and 4 cups broth. Bring to a boil; cover and simmer 1 hour and 30 minutes. Meanwhile, cook rice according to package directions, using chicken broth instead of water.

3. Cook bacon in a skillet over medium heat, turning once, 5 minutes or until crisp. Remove bacon, and drain on paper towels, reserving 2 Tbsp. drippings in skillet. Crumble bacon. Cook bell pepper and next 2 ingredients in hot drippings, stirring often, 10 minutes. Transfer to a large bowl. Stir in salt and pepper.

4. Preheat oven to 350°. Grate cheese on the large holes of a box grater.

5. Remove black-eyed peas from broth using a slotted spoon. (You should have about 3 cups peas.) Discard broth. Add peas to bell pepper mixture. Add rice, crumbled bacon, and 1 cup cheese. Stir gently to combine. Transfer to a lightly greased 11- x 7-inch baking dish or divide among 6 lightly greased (10-oz.) ramekins. Top with remaining cheese.

6. Bake at 350° for 15 minutes or until cheese is melted. Serve immediately. (Serves 6)

serve it on the side

Okra-and-Corn Maque Choux: Sauté ¼ lb. diced spicy smoked sausage in a large skillet over medium-high heat 3 minutes or until browned. Add ½ cup chopped sweet onion, ½ cup chopped green bell pepper, and 2 minced garlic cloves, and sauté 5 minutes or until tender. Add 3 cups fresh corn kernels; 1 cup sliced fresh okra; and 1 cup peeled, seeded, and diced tomato. Cook, stirring often, 10 minutes. Season with table salt and freshly ground black pepper to taste. (Serves 8)

Sweet Onion Casserole

Georgia is known for its Vidalias, a sweet onion without the hot bite of red, yellow, or brown varieties. Paired with rice and cheese, the Vidalia makes a surprisingly succulent springtime side.

¾ cup uncooked long-grain rice

3¾ cups chopped sweet onion

2 Tbsp. canola oil

1 Tbsp. all-purpose flour

½ tsp. kosher salt

1 cup fat-free milk

3 oz. Gruyère cheese, shredded
   (about ¾ cup)

Vegetable cooking spray

¼ cup (1 oz.) grated fresh
   Parmesan cheese

2 Tbsp. chopped fresh parsley

HANDS-ON: 26 MIN.   ✦   **TOTAL:** 1 HR.

1. Preheat oven to 350°.

2. Bring 1 qt. water to a boil; stir in rice. Cook 5 minutes; drain. Set aside.

3. Sauté onions in hot oil in a large skillet over medium-high heat 5 to 6 minutes or until tender, stirring occasionally. Whisk in flour and salt until smooth. Cook 1 minute, whisking constantly.

4. Gradually add milk, stirring with a whisk until blended. Cook 3 minutes or until thick, stirring frequently. Add Gruyère cheese and rice, stirring until cheese melts. Pour onion mixture into an 11- x 7-inch baking dish coated with cooking spray. Sprinkle with Parmesan cheese.

5. Bake, uncovered, at 350° for 35 minutes or until bubbly and brown. Sprinkle with parsley. (Serves 8)

Sweet Potato Spoonbread

The method for this spoonbread includes beating egg whites and folding them into the sweet potato mixture. The air whipped into the egg whites acts as the leavening agent—similar to a soufflé—while the cornmeal helps the spoonbread stand up, even after you start serving it.

2½ cups milk

1 Tbsp. fresh thyme leaves

2 tsp. sea salt

½ tsp. freshly ground black
    pepper

Pinch of ground red pepper

1 cup plain yellow cornmeal

6 Tbsp. butter

3 medium-size sweet potatoes,
    baked, peeled, and mashed

5 large eggs, separated

2 tsp. baking powder

HANDS-ON: 1 HR. ✦ **TOTAL:** 2 HR.

1. Preheat oven to 350°. Bring first 5 ingredients to a simmer in a 3-qt. saucepan over medium heat. Whisk cornmeal into milk mixture in a slow, steady stream. Cook, whisking constantly, 2 to 3 minutes or until mixture thickens and pulls away from bottom of pan. Remove from heat, and stir in butter. Cool 10 minutes.

2. Place potatoes in bowl; stir in cornmeal mixture. Stir in egg yolks and baking powder, stirring until well blended. Beat egg whites at high speed with an electric mixer until soft peaks form; fold into potato mixture. Spoon into a well-greased 3-qt. baking dish.

3. Bake at 350° for 40 to 45 minutes or until golden brown and puffy. (Edges will be firm and center will still be slightly soft.) Cool 10 minutes on a wire rack before serving. (Serves 8 to 10)

Fresh Corn Spoonbread

Although they're called "breads," spoonbreads are moist and should have the consistency of a savory pudding. Most, such as this corn spoonbread, include cornmeal, and are so soft and creamy. They must be eaten with a fork or spoon—hence the name.

1 cup self-rising white
    cornmeal mix
½ cup all-purpose flour
2 Tbsp. sugar
1 tsp. table salt
4 cups fresh corn kernels
    (about 8 ears)
2 cups plain yogurt
¼ cup butter, melted
¼ cup chopped fresh chives
2 Tbsp. chopped fresh parsley
1 tsp. minced fresh thyme
3 large eggs, lightly beaten
Garnish: chopped fresh chives

HANDS-ON: 5 MIN. ✦ **TOTAL:** 1 HR., 5 MIN.

1. Preheat oven to 350°. Stir together first 4 ingredients in a large bowl; make a well in center of mixture. Stir together corn and next 6 ingredients; add to cornmeal mixture, stirring just until dry ingredients are moistened. Divide mixture among 12 (6-oz.) greased ramekins.

2. Bake at 350° for 35 to 40 minutes or until golden brown and set. Serve immediately. (Serves 12)

Tomato Pie with Bacon and Cheddar

Celebrate summer with this savory pie full of fresh red fruit. Don't forget to drain the bacon so the grease ends up on the paper towel and not on your plate. If you are short on time, use a prepared crust rather than making your own.

CRUST

2½ cups self-rising soft-wheat
    flour (such as White Lily)

1 cup cold butter, cut up

8 cooked bacon slices, chopped

¾ cup sour cream

FILLING

2¾ lb. assorted large tomatoes,
    divided

2 tsp. kosher salt, divided

1½ cups (6 oz.) freshly shredded
    extra-sharp Cheddar cheese

½ cup freshly shredded
    Parmigiano-Reggiano cheese

½ cup mayonnaise

1 large egg, lightly beaten

2 Tbsp. fresh dill sprigs

1 Tbsp. chopped fresh chives

1 Tbsp. chopped fresh flat-leaf
    parsley

1 Tbsp. apple cider vinegar

1 green onion, thinly sliced

2 tsp. sugar

¼ tsp. freshly ground black
    pepper

1½ Tbsp. plain yellow cornmeal

Garnishes: fresh basil leaves,
    fresh parsley, chopped green
    onions, fresh dill

HANDS-ON: 45 MIN. ✦ **TOTAL:** 3 HR.

1. **Prepare Crust:** Place flour in bowl of a heavy-duty electric stand mixer; cut in cold butter with a pastry blender or fork until crumbly. Chill 10 minutes. Add bacon to flour mixture; beat at low speed just until combined. Gradually add sour cream, ¼ cup at a time, beating just until blended after each addition.

2. Spoon mixture onto a heavily floured surface; sprinkle lightly with flour, and knead 3 or 4 times, adding more flour as needed. Roll to a 13-inch round. Gently place dough in a 9-inch fluted tart pan with 2-inch sides and a removable bottom. Press dough into pan; trim off excess dough along edges. Chill 30 minutes.

3. **Prepare Filling:** Cut 2 lb. tomatoes into ¼-inch-thick slices, and remove seeds. Place tomatoes in a single layer on paper towels; sprinkle with 1 tsp. salt. Let stand 30 minutes.

4. Preheat oven to 425°. Stir together Cheddar cheese and mayonnaise, next 9 ingredients, and remaining 1 tsp. salt in a large bowl until combined.

5. Pat tomato slices dry with a paper towel. Sprinkle cornmeal over bottom of crust. Lightly spread ½ cup cheese mixture onto crust; layer with half of tomato slices in slightly overlapping rows. Spread with ½ cup cheese mixture. Repeat layers, using remaining tomato slices and cheese mixture. Cut remaining ¾ lb. tomatoes into ¼-inch-thick slices, and arrange on top of pie.

6. Bake at 425° for 40 to 45 minutes, shielding edges with aluminum foil during last 20 minutes to prevent excessive browning. Let stand 1 to 2 hours before serving. (Serves 6 to 8)

Butternut Squash Gratin

Butternut squash is available during the winter months, and the sweet, orange flesh is ideal for baking. The flavor pairs nicely with cinnamon, nutmeg, and potatoes, which you should slice by layer as you go— or at the very least set them aside in water. Otherwise, potatoes sliced in advance may turn brown.

1 (3-lb.) butternut squash

1 (3-lb.) spaghetti squash

2 Tbsp. butter, melted

1 cup firmly packed light brown
    sugar, divided

½ tsp. ground cinnamon

¼ tsp. ground nutmeg

3 cups whipping cream

5 large Yukon gold potatoes
    (about 2½ lb.)

1 tsp. table salt

1 tsp. freshly ground black
    pepper

4 cups (16 oz.) freshly shredded
    fontina cheese*

HANDS-ON: 45 MIN. ✦ **TOTAL:** 3 HR., 30 MIN.

1. Preheat oven to 450°. Cut butternut and spaghetti squash in half lengthwise; remove and discard seeds. Place squash, cut sides up, in a lightly greased 17- x 12-inch jelly-roll pan. Drizzle with butter, and sprinkle with ½ cup brown sugar. Bake 40 minutes or until tender. Cool 20 minutes.

2. Using a fork, scrape inside of spaghetti squash to remove spaghetti-like strands, and place in a large bowl. Scoop pulp from butternut squash; coarsely chop pulp, and toss with spaghetti squash.

3. Stir together cinnamon, nutmeg, and remaining ½ cup brown sugar.

4. Cook cream in a heavy non-aluminum saucepan over medium heat, stirring often, 5 minutes or just until it begins to steam (do not boil); remove from heat.

5. Using a mandoline, cut potatoes into ⅛-inch-thick slices. Arrange one-fourth of potato slices in a thin layer on bottom of a greased 13- x 9-inch baking dish. Spoon one-third of squash mixture over potatoes (squash layer should be about ¼-inch thick); sprinkle with ¼ tsp. salt, ¼ tsp. pepper, 1 cup fontina cheese, and ¾ cup hot cream. Repeat layers twice, sprinkling one-third of sugar mixture over each of second and third squash layers. (Do not sprinkle sugar mixture over first squash layer.) Top with remaining potato slices, ¼ tsp. salt, and ¼ tsp. pepper. Gently press layers down with back of a spoon. Sprinkle top with remaining 1 cup cheese and ¾ cup hot cream; sprinkle with remaining brown sugar mixture. Place baking dish on an aluminum foil-lined baking sheet.

6. Bake, covered with foil, at 450° for 1 hour; uncover and bake 25 more minutes or until golden brown and potatoes are tender. Cool on a wire rack 20 minutes before serving. (Serves 8)

* Gouda cheese may be substituted.

Parmesan Corn Pudding

This is ideal for those months when fresh corn isn't at its peak—it makes use of frozen corn instead. The combination of pureed and whole corn gives the dish a creamy texture and a boost of sweet flavor.

2 (12-oz.) packages frozen white shoe peg corn, thawed and divided
⅓ cup sugar
¼ cup all-purpose flour
2 Tbsp. plain yellow cornmeal
½ tsp. table salt
6 Tbsp. butter, melted
1½ cups milk
4 large eggs
2 Tbsp. chopped fresh chives
½ cup (2 oz.) shredded Parmesan cheese

HANDS-ON: 15 MIN. ✦ **TOTAL:** 55 MIN.

1. Preheat oven to 350°. Place 1 package of corn and next 7 ingredients in a large food processor. Process until smooth, stopping to scrape down sides.

2. Transfer mixture to a large bowl; stir in chives and remaining corn. Pour mixture into a lightly greased 2-qt. baking dish; sprinkle with cheese.

3. Bake at 350° for 40 to 45 minutes or until set. (Serves 8)

Pimiento Cheese Creamed Spinach

Creamed spinach takes a trip to the South when mixed with pimientos and sharp Cheddar cheese.

3 (10-oz.) packages frozen chopped spinach, thawed
2 Tbsp. unsalted butter
½ medium-size yellow onion, finely chopped
3 garlic cloves, minced
4 oz. cream cheese, cut into small pieces and softened
1 cup milk
1 (8-oz.) container sour cream
¼ cup mayonnaise
1 Tbsp. Dijon mustard
1 large egg, lightly beaten
1 (4-oz.) jar diced pimiento, drained and rinsed
2 cups (8 oz.) shredded sharp Cheddar cheese, divided
Vegetable cooking spray
1½ tsp. kosher salt
½ tsp. freshly ground black pepper
½ cup panko (Japanese breadcrumbs)
2 Tbsp. unsalted butter, melted

HANDS-ON: 30 MIN.   ✦   **TOTAL:** 1 HR., 20 MIN.

1. Preheat oven to 350°. Drain spinach well, pressing between paper towels. Melt 2 Tbsp. butter in a large Dutch oven over medium heat. Add onion, and sauté 5 minutes or until tender. Add garlic, and sauté 1 minute; remove from heat.

2. Stir cream cheese into onion mixture until melted and well blended. Stir in spinach, milk, and next 3 ingredients. Stir together egg, pimiento, and 1½ cups cheese; stir egg mixture into spinach mixture. Spoon mixture into a 2-qt. baking dish coated with cooking spray; sprinkle with salt and pepper.

3. Toss together panko, 2 Tbsp. melted butter, and remaining ½ cup Cheddar cheese; sprinkle over spinach mixture.

4. Bake at 350° for 50 minutes or until bubbly and golden. (Serves 8)

Caramelized Onion Mashed Potato Bake

Caramelizing onions adds a sweet umami flavor to this mashed potato bake. Just be sure to caramelize them correctly—go for thick slices (about ⅛-inch), in a mix of oil and butter, over medium-low for about 45 minutes. Your final step should be to deglaze the pan to loosen all the yummy brown bits and goodness.

4 lb. russet potatoes

3 tsp. table salt, divided

1¼ cups warm buttermilk

½ cup warm milk

¼ cup melted butter

½ tsp. freshly ground black
   pepper

1¼ cups freshly grated Gruyère
   cheese

1 cup chopped caramelized
   onions

2 Tbsp. chopped fresh parsley

HANDS-ON: 25 MIN.   ✦   **TOTAL:** 50 MIN.

1. Preheat oven to 350°. Peel potatoes; cut into 2-inch pieces. Bring potatoes, 2 tsp. salt, and water to cover to a boil in a large Dutch oven over medium-high heat; boil 20 minutes or until tender. Drain. Return potatoes to Dutch oven, reduce heat to low, and cook, stirring occasionally, 3 to 5 minutes or until potatoes are dry.

2. Mash potatoes with a potato masher to desired consistency. Stir in warm buttermilk, warm milk, melted butter, pepper, and remaining 1 tsp. salt, stirring just until blended.

3. Stir in Gruyère cheese, caramelized onions, and parsley, and spoon the mixture into a lightly greased 2½-qt. baking dish or 8 (10-oz.) ramekins. Bake at 350° for 35 minutes. (Serves 6 to 8)

dress it up

Go pig or go home: Crispy prosciutto comes together in seconds. Arrange half 1 (4-oz.) package of prosciutto on a paper towel-lined microwave-safe plate; cover with a paper towel. Microwave at HIGH 2 minutes or until crisp. Repeat procedure with remaining prosciutto. Break prosciutto into large pieces, and crumble on top of mashed potato bake.

Chipotle Scalloped Potatoes

Chipotle peppers are actually dried smoked jalapeños. They're often canned in adobo sauce—a thick red paste made of ground chiles, herbs, and vinegar—and can pack quite a punch of heat. If you prefer less spice, skip the chopped pepper and include the adobo sauce only.

½ cup half-and-half

2 garlic cloves, chopped

1 canned chipotle pepper in
    adobo sauce

1½ tsp. kosher salt

½ tsp. freshly ground black
    pepper

⅛ tsp. ground nutmeg

2½ cups whipping cream

Vegetable cooking spray

3 lb. russet potatoes, peeled
    and cut into ⅛-inch slices

1 cup (4 oz.) shredded sharp
    white Cheddar cheese

4 cooked bacon slices,
    crumbled

Garnish: chopped fresh
    chives

HANDS-ON: 30 MIN.   ✦   **TOTAL:** 1 HR., 50 MIN.

1. Preheat oven to 400°. Process first 6 ingredients in a blender or food processor until smooth. Transfer mixture to a medium bowl, and stir in whipping cream.

2. Lightly grease a 13- x 9-inch baking dish with cooking spray. Spread one-fourth of potatoes in a single layer in prepared dish; top with one-fourth of cream mixture. Repeat layers three more times with remaining potatoes and cream mixture.

3. Bake, covered, at 400° for 50 minutes. Uncover and sprinkle with cheese and bacon. Bake 20 more minutes or until lightly browned and bubbly. Let stand 10 minutes. (Serves 8 to 10)

Two-Potato Gratin

Craving sweet potato casserole and scalloped potatoes? This dish provides the best of both sweet and savory all in one.

2 shallots, diced

¼ cup butter, divided

2 cups heavy cream

2 Tbsp. chopped parsley

1 Tbsp. chopped chives

1 tsp. kosher salt

½ tsp. ground white pepper

⅛ tsp. freshly grated nutmeg

1½ lb. Yukon gold potatoes

1½ lb. sweet potatoes

2 cups milk

1½ cups (6 oz.) shredded
   Gruyère cheese

¼ cup grated Parmesan cheese

HANDS-ON: 45 MIN.   ✦   **TOTAL:** 1 HR., 45 MIN.

1. Preheat oven to 375°. Sauté shallots in 3 Tbsp. melted butter in a saucepan over medium heat 2 minutes. Stir in cream and next 5 ingredients; cook 2 minutes. Remove from heat; cool 15 minutes.

2. Meanwhile, peel and thinly slice all potatoes. Combine sliced potatoes and milk in a large, microwave-safe bowl. Cover with plastic wrap, and microwave at HIGH 5 minutes. Uncover and gently stir mixture. Re-cover and microwave 5 more minutes. Drain mixture, discarding milk.

3. Layer one-third of Yukon gold potatoes in a well-greased (with butter) 13- x 9-inch baking dish; top with one-third of sweet potatoes. Spoon one-third of cream mixture over potatoes, and sprinkle with ½ cup Gruyère cheese. Repeat layers twice, and top with Parmesan cheese. Cut remaining 1 Tbsp. butter into small pieces, and dot over top. Cover with aluminum foil.

4. Bake at 375° for 30 minutes. Uncover; bake 20 minutes or until browned. Let stand 10 minutes. (Serves 10 to 12)

Classic Parmesan Scalloped Potatoes

Stirring these spuds every 10 minutes throughout the cooking process is the key to a creamy, evenly cooked dish.

2 lb. Yukon gold potatoes, peeled and thinly sliced
3 cups whipping cream
¼ cup chopped fresh flat-leaf parsley
2 garlic cloves, chopped
1½ tsp. table salt
¼ tsp. freshly ground black pepper
½ cup grated Parmesan cheese

HANDS-ON: 20 MIN.   ✦   **TOTAL:** 1 HR., 15 MIN.

1. Preheat oven to 400°. Layer potatoes in a 13- x 9-inch or 3-qt. baking dish.

2. Stir together cream and next 4 ingredients in a large bowl. Pour cream mixture over potatoes.

3. Bake at 400° for 30 minutes, stirring gently every 10 minutes. Sprinkle with cheese; bake 15 to 20 more minutes or until bubbly and golden brown. Let stand on a wire rack 10 minutes before serving. (Serves 8 to 10)

mix it up

Gruyère Scalloped Potatoes: Substitute finely shredded Gruyère cheese for Parmesan. Reduce parsley to 2 Tbsp. and table salt to 1 tsp. Prepare recipe as directed, stirring 1 tsp. freshly ground Italian seasoning into cream mixture in Step 2. (Serves 8 to 10)

Note: *We tested with McCormick Italian Herb Seasoning Grinder.*

Creamy Spinach Mashed Potato Bake

This dish has the three C's covered: Spinach provides color, pecans add crunch, and garlic-and-herb cheese gives it a creamy finish.

4 lb. russet potatoes

3 tsp. table salt, divided

1¼ cups warm buttermilk

½ cup warm milk

¼ cup melted butter

½ tsp. freshly ground black pepper

1 (5-oz.) package fresh baby spinach, cooked until wilted

1 (5.5-oz.) package buttery garlic-and-herb spreadable cheese

¼ cup chopped toasted pecans

HANDS-ON: 25 MIN.   ✦   **TOTAL:** 50 MIN.

1. Preheat oven to 350°. Peel potatoes; cut into 2-inch pieces. Bring potatoes, 2 tsp. salt, and water to cover to a boil in a large Dutch oven over medium-high heat; boil 20 minutes or until tender. Drain. Return potatoes to Dutch oven, reduce heat to low, and cook, stirring occasionally, 3 to 5 minutes or until potatoes are dry.

2. Mash potatoes with a potato masher to desired consistency. Stir in warm buttermilk, warm milk, melted butter, pepper, and remaining 1 tsp. salt, stirring just until blended.

3. Stir in spinach, cheese, and pecans, and spoon the mixture into a lightly greased 2½-qt. baking dish or 8 (10-oz.) ramekins. Bake at 350° for 35 minutes. (Serves 6 to 8)

Cornflake, Pecan, and Marshmallow-Topped Sweet Potato Casserole

Marshmallows have long been the preferred topping for sweet potato casserole. But adding cornflakes and a sweet pecan-brown sugar blend to the mix gives this traditional casserole an extra crispiness and crunch you'll go back to time after time.

SWEET POTATO FILLING

2½ lbs. sweet potatoes (about
    5 medium)

2 Tbsp. butter, softened

½ cup firmly packed brown
    sugar

½ cup 2% reduced-fat milk

1 large egg

½ tsp. table salt

½ tsp. vanilla extract

Vegetable cooking spray

**CORNFLAKE, PECAN,
AND MARSHMALLOW
TOPPING**

1¼ cups cornflakes cereal,
    crushed

¼ cup chopped pecans

1 Tbsp. brown sugar

1 Tbsp. melted butter

1¼ cups miniature marshmallows

HANDS-ON: 10 MIN.   ✦   **TOTAL:** 2 HR., 30 MIN.

1. **Prepare Filling:** Preheat oven to 400°. Bake sweet potatoes on a baking sheet 1 hour or until tender. Reduce oven temperature to 350°. Let potatoes stand until cool to touch (about 20 minutes); peel and mash with a potato masher.

2. Beat mashed sweet potatoes, 2 Tbsp. softened butter, and next 5 ingredients at medium speed with an electric mixer until smooth. Spoon mixture into an 11- x 7-inch baking dish coated with cooking spray.

3. **Prepare Topping:** Stir together crushed cornflakes cereal and next 3 ingredients. Sprinkle over sweet potato mixture.

4. Bake at 350° for 30 minutes. Remove from oven; let stand 10 minutes. Sprinkle miniature marshmallows over cornflake mixture, and bake 10 more minutes. (Serves 8)

mix it up

Golden Meringue-Topped Sweet Potato Casserole: Omit Cornflake, Pecan, and Marshmallow Topping. Bake Sweet Potato Filling at 350° for 30 minutes. Remove from oven; let stand 10 minutes. Beat 4 egg whites at high speed with an electric mixer until foamy. Gradually add ¼ cup granulated sugar, 1 Tbsp. at a time, beating until stiff peaks form and sugar is dissolved. Spread meringue over sweet potato mixture; bake 10 more minutes or until golden. (Serves 8)

Truffled Mac and Cheese

White truffle oil has an intense earthy flavor that punches up ordinary mac and cheese. Be sure to splurge on the truffle oil: It's worth it.

2¼ cups 1% low-fat milk, divided

2 cups sliced onion

1 bay leaf

12 oz. uncooked elbow macaroni

2 Tbsp. all-purpose flour

¾ tsp. kosher salt

¾ cup fontina cheese, shredded

½ cup Comté or Gruyère cheese, shredded

1½ tsp. white truffle oil

2 oz. French bread baguette, torn

2 Tbsp. grated fresh Parmesan cheese

2 garlic cloves, crushed

1 Tbsp. olive oil

HANDS-ON: 36 MIN. ✦ **TOTAL:** 44 MIN.

1. Heat 1¾ cups milk, onion, and bay leaf in a large saucepan to 180° or until tiny bubbles form around edges (do not boil). Cover and remove from heat; let stand 15 minutes.

2. Cook pasta according to package directions; drain.

3. Pour milk mixture through a wire-mesh strainer into a serving bowl; discard solids. Return milk to saucepan over medium heat. Combine remaining ½ cup milk and flour in a small bowl, stirring with a whisk until well blended. Gradually stir flour mixture and salt into warm milk, stirring constantly with a whisk. Bring mixture to a boil, stirring frequently; cook 1 minute, stirring constantly. Remove from heat; let stand 6 minutes or until mixture cools to 155°. Gradually add fontina and Comté cheeses, stirring until cheeses melt. Stir in pasta and truffle oil. Spoon mixture into a 2-qt. broiler-safe glass or ceramic baking dish.

4. Preheat broiler. Place bread, Parmesan cheese, and garlic in a food processor; process until coarse crumbs form. Drizzle with olive oil; pulse until fine crumbs form. Sprinkle breadcrumb mixture over pasta. Place dish on middle rack in oven; broil 2 minutes or until golden brown. (Serves 6)

Four-Cheese Macaroni

The more cheese the merrier! Not a fan of one of these cheeses? Swap them out for one of your favorites—just be sure to pick ones that melt well without creating excess oil. And grate the cheeses yourself—they'll melt easier and create a creamier dish.

12 oz. cavatappi pasta or
    macaroni
½ cup butter
½ cup all-purpose flour
½ tsp. ground red pepper
3 cups milk
2 cups (8 oz.) freshly shredded
    white Cheddar cheese
1 cup (4 oz.) freshly shredded
    Monterey Jack cheese
1 cup (4 oz.) freshly shredded
    fontina cheese
1 cup (4 oz.) freshly shredded
    Asiago cheese
1½ cups soft, fresh breadcrumbs
½ cup chopped cooked bacon
½ cup chopped pecans
2 Tbsp. butter, melted

HANDS-ON: 40 MIN. ✦ **TOTAL:** 1 HR., 15 MIN.

1. Preheat oven to 350°. Prepare pasta according to package directions; drain.

2. Meanwhile, melt ½ cup butter in a Dutch oven over low heat; whisk in flour and ground red pepper until smooth. Cook, whisking constantly, 1 minute. Gradually whisk in milk; cook over medium heat, whisking constantly, 6 to 7 minutes or until milk mixture is thickened and bubbly. Remove from heat.

3. Toss together Cheddar cheese and next 3 ingredients in a medium bowl; reserve 1½ cups cheese mixture. Add remaining cheese mixture and hot cooked pasta to sauce, tossing to coat. Spoon into a lightly greased 13- x 9-inch baking dish. Top with reserved 1½ cups cheese mixture.

4. Toss together breadcrumbs and next 3 ingredients; sprinkle over cheese mixture.

5. Bake at 350° for 35 to 40 minutes or until bubbly and golden brown. (Serves 8)

The City and the Country Mac and Cheese

Smoky cubes of brined "city" ham mixed with salty bits of "country" ham give this mac and cheese its name and savory appeal. Pasta enveloped in a creamy sauce and melting pockets of gooey cheese take it over the top.

12 oz. elbow macaroni or
    cavatappi pasta
4 cups diced smoked, fully
    cooked ham
1 cup diced country ham
2 Tbsp. vegetable oil
6 Tbsp. butter
⅓ cup grated onion
2 tsp. dry mustard
½ tsp. kosher salt
¼ tsp. freshly ground black
    pepper
¼ tsp. freshly grated nutmeg
⅛ tsp. ground red pepper
5 Tbsp. all-purpose flour
3½ cups milk
1¾ cups heavy cream
2 tsp. prepared horseradish
2 tsp. Worcestershire sauce
2 cups (8 oz.) shredded extra-
    sharp Cheddar cheese
2 cups diced Gruyère or Swiss
    cheese
1½ cups soft, fresh breadcrumbs
    (about 4 white bread slices)
2 Tbsp. butter, melted
1 Tbsp. minced fresh chives

HANDS-ON: 40 MIN. ✦ **TOTAL:** 1 HR., 25 MIN.

1. Preheat oven to 350°. Prepare pasta according to package directions for al dente; drain.

2. Stir together smoked ham and country ham. Sauté half of ham mixture in 1 Tbsp. hot oil in a large skillet 7 to 8 minutes or until lightly browned. Repeat with remaining ham mixture and oil.

3. Melt 6 Tbsp. butter in a large saucepan over medium heat. Add onion and next 5 ingredients, and sauté 30 seconds or until fragrant. Add flour, and cook, stirring constantly, 2 minutes or until golden brown and smooth. Gradually whisk in milk and cream, and bring to a boil, whisking occasionally. Reduce heat to medium-low, and simmer, whisking constantly, 5 minutes or until slightly thickened and mixture coats a spoon. Stir in horseradish and Worcestershire sauce. Remove from heat, and stir in Cheddar cheese until melted. Stir in pasta, ham, and Gruyère; pour into a lightly greased 13- x 9-inch baking dish.

4. Process breadcrumbs and 2 Tbsp. melted butter in a food processor 6 to 7 seconds to combine. Sprinkle over pasta mixture.

5. Bake on an aluminum foil-lined jelly-roll pan at 350° for 30 minutes or until bubbly and golden. Remove from oven to a wire rack, and cool 15 minutes. Top with chives. (Serves 8 to 10)

NOTE: *We tested with Cracker Barrel Extra Sharp Cheddar.*

serve it on the side

Tipsy Berries: Stir together 1 (16-oz.) container fresh strawberries, sliced; 1 cup fresh blueberries; ½ cup fresh raspberries; ¼ cup shaved fresh coconut; 2 Tbsp. bourbon; and 2 tsp. sugar; let stand 10 minutes. Serve with a slotted spoon. (Makes 2½ cups)

Shrimp and Grits Dressing

In the South we serve dressing—mostly varieties of cornbread dressing. And this twist on another Southern staple proves we aren't afraid to re-imagine most any dish as a form of this traditional holiday side.

1 lb. peeled, medium-size raw
    shrimp

3 cups chicken broth

½ tsp. table salt

¼ tsp. ground red pepper

1 cup uncooked regular grits

½ cup butter

3 large eggs, lightly beaten

1 red bell pepper, diced

1 cup fine, dry breadcrumbs

1 cup chopped green onions

½ cup grated Parmesan cheese

HANDS-ON: 35 MIN. ✦ **TOTAL:** 1 HR., 50 MIN.

1. Preheat oven to 325°. Devein shrimp, if desired.

2. Bring broth and next 2 ingredients to a boil in a large saucepan over medium-high heat. Whisk in grits, and return to a boil; reduce heat to low, and stir in butter. Cover and simmer, stirring occasionally, 10 minutes or until liquid is absorbed. Remove from heat.

3. Stir together eggs and next 4 ingredients in a large bowl. Gradually stir about one-fourth of hot grits mixture into egg mixture; add egg mixture to remaining hot grits mixture, stirring constantly. Stir in shrimp until blended. Pour grits mixture into a lightly greased 11- x 7-inch baking dish.

4. Bake at 325° for 55 minutes to 1 hour or until mixture is set. Let stand 10 minutes. (Serves 6 to 8)

Cornbread Dressing

This Southern staple yields one large and one small pan. That means you can freeze one for later and get ahead without even trying. To freeze: Prepare recipe as directed through Step 5 and cover with plastic wrap and a container lid. When you're ready to cook, simply thaw the dressing in the fridge overnight, let it stand at room temperature for 30 minutes, and bake, uncovered, at 400° for 35 to 40 minutes or until golden.

1 cup butter, divided

3 cups self-rising white
  cornmeal mix

1 cup all-purpose flour

7 large eggs, divided

3 cups buttermilk

3 cups soft, fresh breadcrumbs

2 large sweet onions, diced

4 celery ribs, diced

¼ cup finely chopped fresh sage

¼ cup finely chopped fresh
  parsley

1 Tbsp. seasoned pepper

7 cups chicken broth

HANDS-ON: 52 MIN. ✦ **TOTAL:** 2 HR., 7 MIN.

1. Preheat oven to 425°. Place ½ cup butter in a 13- x 9-inch pan; heat in oven at 425° for 4 minutes. Stir together cornmeal and flour; whisk in 3 eggs and buttermilk.

2. Pour hot butter into batter, and stir until blended. Pour batter into pan.

3. Bake at 425° for 30 minutes or until golden brown. Cool. Crumble cornbread into a large bowl; stir in breadcrumbs, and set aside. Reduce oven temperature to 400°.

4. Melt remaining ½ cup butter in a skillet over medium heat; add onions and celery, and sauté 5 minutes. Stir in sage, parsley, and seasoned pepper; sauté 1 minute. Remove from heat, and stir into cornbread mixture.

5. Whisk together chicken broth and remaining 4 eggs; stir into cornbread mixture. Pour into 1 lightly greased 13- x 9-inch pan and 1 lightly greased 8-inch square pan.

6. Bake at 400° for 35 to 40 minutes or until golden brown. (Serves 16 to 18)

mix it up

Chorizo-and-Dried Cherry Dressing: Sauté ¾ lb. diced chorizo sausage in 1 Tbsp. hot oil in a large skillet over medium-high heat 4 to 5 minutes or until browned; drain. Prepare recipe as directed, stirring sausage and 1½ cups coarsely chopped dried cherries into breadcrumbs in Step 3. (Serves 16 to 18)

MASTER IT the FIRST TIME

CAST-IRON SKILLET

All it takes is a little love and care to make your cast-iron skillet last forever.

REVIVING AND RE-SEASONING

Seasoning is the process of oiling and heating old or rusted cast iron to protect its porous surface from moisture. When the pan is heated, the oil is absorbed, creating a nonstick surface.

1. Rinse the skillet in hot, sudsy water. Dry the skillet well with a towel.

2. Rub the skillet generously with vegetable oil, coating both the insides and the bottom of the skillet.

3. Place the skillet in an oven, and bake at 350° for 2 hours. Let the skillet cool, and pour off any excess oil. Repeat this process two or three times to season the skillet completely.

RUST AND ACID VS. CAST IRON

- To rid your skillet of rust stains, rub a handy rust eraser on the stain, and then re-season the pan. You can find rust erasers at hardware stores, bike shops, or woodworking shops. Or, use fine steel wool. Scrub the skillet with hot water, and then scour with fine steel wool again before drying and re-seasoning.

- Never marinate in cast iron. Acidic mixtures will damage the seasoning. Re-season if food particles start to stick, rust appears, or you experience a metallic taste. And never put a cast-iron skillet in the dishwasher. Moist environments will cause rust and damage the seasoning.

Follow these steps every time you cook in your cast iron.

1. Apply vegetable oil to the cooking surface, and preheat the skillet on low heat, increasing the temperature slowly.

2. Because acids can corrode cast-iron, remove any highly acidic foods (such as tomatoes) from the skillet as soon as the dish has finished cooking.

3. As soon as you remove the food from the skillet, scrub the pan while it's still warm (but cool enough to handle) under hot water. Use a stiff brush or plastic scrubber. Kosher salt is also a good scrubbing agent for baked-on bits. Never use soap unless you're re-seasoning.

4. After scrubbing the pan under hot water, place on warm burner for a few minutes to dry. After it's dry, drizzle a little bit of oil on the inside of the skillet to help it maintain the seasoning. Rub the oil all over the skillet with a paper towel so that the skillet shines. Let the skillet cool completely.

Oyster Dressing

The key to this oyster dressing is the cornbread. It's prepared in a hot skillet coated with bacon drippings—a step you simply can't skip. The bacon drippings add tons of flavor to the cornbread, and ultimately the dressing.

2 medium onions, diced

4 celery ribs, diced

2 red bell peppers, diced

2 green bell peppers, diced

4 garlic cloves, minced

¼ cup olive oil

2 (8-oz.) containers fresh
    oysters, drained and coarsely
    chopped

⅔ cup dry white wine

½ cup chicken broth

¼ cup butter

3 bay leaves

2 Tbsp. fresh thyme leaves

2 tsp. freshly ground black
    pepper

1 tsp. table salt

1 tsp. crushed dried red pepper

1 tsp. hot pepper sauce

2 large eggs

½ cup grated Parmesan cheese

Sizzlin' Skillet Cornbread,
    crumbled

HANDS-ON: 30 MIN. ✦ **TOTAL:** 2 HR., 5 MIN., INCLUDING CORNBREAD

1. Preheat oven to 375°. Sauté first 5 ingredients in hot oil in a large skillet over medium heat 15 to 20 minutes or until tender and lightly browned. Stir in oysters and next 9 ingredients; cook 3 to 4 minutes or until edges of oysters begin to curl. Remove from heat; let stand 10 minutes. Remove and discard bay leaves.

2. Place mixture in a large bowl; stir in eggs and cheese. Fold in cornbread. Place mixture in a lightly greased 13- x 9-inch baking dish.

3. Bake at 375° for 40 to 45 minutes or until lightly browned. (Serves 8)

NOTE: *To make ahead, prepare recipe as directed through Step 2. Cover tightly, and freeze up to one month. Thaw in refrigerator 24 hours. Let stand at room temperature 30 minutes. Proceed with recipe as directed.*

Sizzlin' Skillet Cornbread

HANDS-ON: 15 MIN. ✦ **TOTAL:** 50 MIN.

2 Tbsp. bacon drippings

2 cups buttermilk

1 large egg

1¾ cups self-rising cornmeal mix

1. Preheat oven to 450°. Coat bottom and sides of a 10-inch cast-iron skillet with bacon drippings; heat in oven 10 minutes.

2. Whisk together remaining ingredients; pour batter into hot skillet.

3. Bake at 450° for 15 minutes or until lightly browned. Invert onto a wire rack. Cool completely (about 30 minutes). (Serves 6)

Savory Bread Pudding with Sage, Mushrooms, and Apple

Another savory bread pudding, this sage, mushroom, and apple combo is ideal served as individual portions. Simply divide the dish into 8-oz. ramekins, and bake at 350° for 25 to 30 minutes for personalized bread puddings.

1 (1-lb.) loaf ciabatta bread, cut
    into 1-inch cubes
½ cup butter, divided
1½ cups chopped sweet onion
¾ cup chopped celery
2 Tbsp. chopped fresh sage
3 (4-oz.) packages wild
    mushroom blend
3 garlic cloves, minced
2 Golden Delicious apples,
    peeled and chopped
2 cups heavy cream
2 cups milk
5 large eggs
1¼ tsp. table salt
¾ tsp. freshly ground black
    pepper
Garnish: fresh sage leaves

HANDS-ON: 25 MIN. ✦ **TOTAL:** 9 HR., 35 MIN., INCLUDING CHILL TIME

1. Preheat oven to 375°. Place bread cubes on a large rimmed baking sheet. Melt ¼ cup butter in a large skillet over low heat. Drizzle melted butter over bread cubes; toss to coat. Bake for 20 minutes or until golden, stirring halfway through. Transfer cubes to a large bowl.

2. Melt 3 Tbsp. butter in skillet over medium-high heat. Add onion and next 4 ingredients to skillet; sauté 12 minutes or until tender. Add mushroom mixture to bread cubes.

3. Melt remaining 1 Tbsp. butter in skillet. Add apple; sauté 4 minutes or until golden. Add apple to bread mixture.

4. Whisk together cream and next 4 ingredients. Pour over bread mixture; toss well. Pour bread mixture into a greased 13- x 9-inch baking dish. Cover and chill at least 8 hours.

5. Preheat oven to 350°. Uncover casserole, and bake for 1 hour and 10 minutes or until set and lightly browned. Let stand 15 minutes. (Serves 12)

Patchwork Cobbler,
page 211

one-dish desserts

The best desserts don't come in a box, a bag, or little plastic sleeves. They come straight out of your baking dish or cast-iron skillet, steaming hot and sugar-crusted. Pies and puddings, cakes and cobblers, Sweet Tea Tiramisù, and syrupy sauces alike come together easily and taste like they took all day.

Winter Blackberry Cobbler

This fruity cobbler takes advantage of the abundance of frozen blackberries during the winter months. If you're lucky enough to have fresh blackberries during the summer, simply sub 8 cups fresh for frozen, and prepare the recipe as directed.

2½ cups all-purpose flour

1¾ tsp. baking powder

¾ tsp. table salt

½ cup shortening

⅔ cup milk

2 cups granulated sugar

⅓ cup all-purpose flour

1 tsp. fresh lemon juice

2 (16-oz.) packages frozen blackberries

¼ cup butter, cut into ¼-inch pieces and divided

1 Tbsp. granulated sugar

HANDS-ON: 45 MIN.   ✦   **TOTAL:** 2 HR., 20 MIN.

1. Preheat oven to 425°.

2. Whisk together first 3 ingredients in a medium bowl. Cut shortening into flour mixture with a pastry blender until mixture is slightly crumbly. Add milk, stirring with a fork until dry ingredients are moistened and mixture is soft enough to form a soft ball.

3. Turn dough out onto a lightly floured surface, and knead 6 to 8 times. Divide dough in half. Roll 1 dough half to ¼-inch thickness on a lightly floured surface, and cut into 1-inch-wide strips. Place on a lightly greased baking sheet.

4. Bake strips at 425° for 15 minutes or until lightly browned. Transfer strips to a wire rack, and cool completely (about 30 minutes). Reduce oven temperature to 350°.

5. Meanwhile, roll remaining dough half to ¼-inch thickness; cut dough into 1-inch-wide strips.

6. Sprinkle 2 cups sugar, ⅓ cup flour, and lemon juice over frozen blackberries in a large bowl, and gently stir.

7. Spoon half of blackberry mixture into a lightly greased 13- x 9-inch baking dish. Break each baked dough strip into 2 or 3 pieces, and place on top of blackberry mixture in baking dish. Dot blackberry mixture with half of butter pieces. Spoon remaining blackberry mixture over baked dough strips.

8. Arrange unbaked dough strips in a lattice design over filling, and sprinkle with 1 Tbsp. sugar. Dot blackberry mixture with remaining butter pieces.

9. Bake at 350° for 50 minutes to 1 hour or until pastry is golden and mixture is bubbly. (Serves 8 to 10)

Apple Cinnamon Dutch Baby

This puffy, light pancake will fall as soon as it leaves the oven, but don't worry, it's still tasty. Be sure to use low-fat or fat-free milk—it will puff higher.

1 large Gala apple, peeled and sliced

1 Tbsp. granulated sugar

3 Tbsp. butter, divided

2 large eggs

½ cup fat-free or low-fat milk

½ cup all-purpose flour, sifted

½ tsp. ground cinnamon

¼ tsp. table salt

¼ tsp. ground nutmeg

1 cup sour cream

½ cup firmly packed light brown sugar

1 to 4 Tbsp. apple cider or orange juice

Garnish: powdered sugar

HANDS-ON: 25 MIN. ✦ **TOTAL:** 45 MIN.

1. Preheat oven to 450°. Heat a 10-inch cast-iron skillet over medium-high heat 5 minutes. Toss together apple slices and sugar in a small bowl. Melt 1 Tbsp. butter in skillet. Add apples, and sauté 5 minutes or until tender. Remove apples from skillet, and wipe skillet clean.

2. Whisk together eggs and milk in a medium bowl. Whisk in flour and next 3 ingredients. Melt remaining 2 Tbsp. butter in skillet over medium-high heat. Immediately pour egg mixture into hot skillet, and top with cooked apples.

3. Bake at 450° for 20 minutes or until pancake is golden and puffed.

4. Meanwhile, stir together sour cream and brown sugar in a small microwave-safe bowl. Microwave at HIGH 45 seconds. Whisk until sugar dissolves. Stir in apple cider. Serve sauce with pancake. (Serves 6)

Patchwork Cobbler *(pictured on page 206)*

A little butter, sugar, and flour are all you need to show off your favorite summer fruits. Dusting the patchwork crust with sugar gives it that extra touch of sweetness.

CRUST

2 cups all-purpose flour

3 Tbsp. granulated sugar

¼ tsp. table salt

1 cup cold butter, cut into pieces

1 large egg yolk

3 Tbsp. ice-cold milk

FILLING

8 cups peeled and sliced firm, ripe peaches (about 7 large or 3 lb.)

6 cups sliced red plums (about 9 medium or 2 lb.)

2 cups fresh blueberries

2 tsp. vanilla extract

1¾ cups granulated sugar

½ cup all-purpose flour

¼ cup butter, melted

1 large egg

Sanding sugar or sparkling sugar

HANDS-ON: 35 MIN.   ✦   **TOTAL:** 3 HR., 30 MIN., INCLUDING CHILL TIME

1. **Prepare Crust:** Stir together first 3 ingredients. Cut 1 cup butter into flour mixture with a pastry blender until mixture resembles coarse meal. Whisk together egg yolk and milk; stir into flour mixture just until dough starts to form a ball. Shape dough into a flat disk using lightly floured hands. Wrap in plastic wrap, and chill 1 to 24 hours.

2. **Prepare Filling:** Preheat oven to 425°. Place peaches and next 3 ingredients in a large bowl. Stir together 1¾ cups sugar and ½ cup flour; sprinkle over peach mixture, and gently stir. Spoon into a greased 13- x 9-inch baking dish. Drizzle with melted butter.

3. Place dough disk on a lightly floured surface; sprinkle with flour. Place a piece of plastic wrap over dough disk. Roll dough to ¼-inch thickness; cut into 2-inch squares. Arrange squares in a patchwork pattern over peach mixture, leaving openings for steam to escape.

4. Whisk together egg and 2 Tbsp. water; brush dough with egg mixture. Sprinkle with sanding sugar or sparkling sugar.

5. Bake on lowest oven rack at 425° for 40 to 55 minutes or until crust is golden and peach mixture is bubbly. Transfer to a wire rack; cool 1 hour. (Serves 10 to 12)

Mini Berry Cobblers

Use a mixture of fresh summer berries for these charming cobblers. When fresh berries aren't in season, frozen work just as well.

18 oz. mixed fresh berries
  (4 cups)
¼ cup granulated sugar
2 Tbsp. butter, melted
1 Tbsp. cornstarch
1½ cups all-purpose flour
⅓ cup granulated sugar
3 Tbsp. minced crystallized
  ginger
2 tsp. baking powder
½ tsp. table salt
⅔ cup cold butter, cubed
½ cup buttermilk
Garnish: fresh mint sprigs

HANDS-ON: 25 MIN.   ✦   **TOTAL:** 1 HR.

1. Preheat oven to 400°.

2. Toss together first 4 ingredients in a medium bowl. Whisk together flour and next 4 ingredients in a large bowl. Cut cold butter into flour mixture with a pastry blender until mixture resembles small peas. Add buttermilk, stirring just until dry ingredients are moistened. Turn dough out onto a lightly floured surface, and knead 3 to 4 times. Pat into a 6- x 4-inch (1-inch-thick) rectangle. Cut into 6 squares; cut squares diagonally into 12 triangles.

3. Arrange 12 (3½-inch) lightly greased miniature cast-iron skillets on an aluminum foil-lined baking sheet. Divide berry mixture among skillets. Place 1 dough triangle over berry mixture in each skillet.

4. Bake at 400° for 20 to 24 minutes or until berry mixture bubbles and crust is golden brown. Cool 15 minutes before serving. Serve warm or at room temperature. (Serves 12)

Pecan-Peach Cobbler

It doesn't get much more Southern than peaches and pecans. This cobbler mixes the two with a twist: The pecans are pressed right into the pastry, making the presentation stand out from other cobblers.

12 to 15 fresh peaches, peeled and sliced (about 16 cups)
3 cups granulated sugar
⅓ cup all-purpose flour
½ tsp. nutmeg
⅔ cup butter
1½ tsp. vanilla extract
2 (14.1-oz.) packages refrigerated piecrusts
½ cup chopped pecans, toasted
¼ cup granulated sugar

HANDS-ON: 40 MIN. ✦ **TOTAL:** 1 HR., 40 MIN.

1. Preheat oven to 475°. Combine first 4 ingredients in a Dutch oven, and let stand 10 minutes or until sugar dissolves. Bring peach mixture to a boil; reduce heat to low, and simmer 10 minutes or until tender. Remove from heat; add butter and vanilla, stirring until butter melts.

2. Unfold 2 piecrusts. Sprinkle ¼ cup pecans and 2 Tbsp. sugar over 1 piecrust; top with other piecrust. Roll into a 12-inch circle, gently pressing pecans into pastry. Cut into 1½-inch strips. Repeat with remaining piecrusts, pecans, and sugar.

3. Spoon half of peach mixture into a lightly greased 13- x 9-inch baking dish. Arrange half of pastry strips in a lattice design over top of peach mixture.

4. Bake at 475° for 20 to 25 minutes or until lightly browned. Spoon remaining peach mixture over baked pastry. Top with remaining pastry strips in a lattice design. Bake 15 to 18 more minutes. Serve warm or cold. (Serves 8 to 10)

MASTER IT
the FIRST TIME

LATTICE PIECRUST

The lattice piecrust looks difficult, but all it takes is a few well-placed folds. Start by rolling out your dough with a rolling pin. Then, using a pizza wheel, pasta cutter, or sharp knife, cut the dough into 10 (½-inch) strips. (See page 20 for more lattice piecrust ideas.)

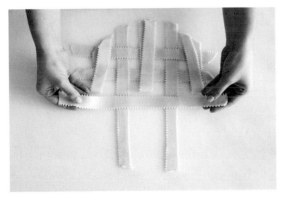

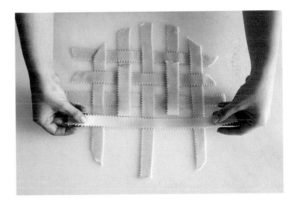

1. Place five strips spaced 1-inch apart over your filling, allowing the excess to hang over. Next, fold the two outside and the center strips up. Place a strip crosswise, and unfold the three vertical strips.

2. Next, fold up only the second and the fourth strips, leaving the center strip down. Place another strip down crosswise, and then unfold the two vertical strips.

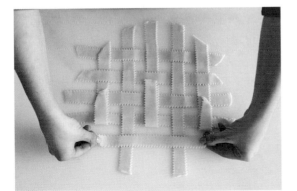

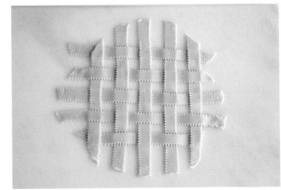

3. Fold the two outside and the center strips up again, and place the final strip down crosswise. Unfold the three vertical strips.

4. If necessary, rotate your pie or cobbler and repeat the steps on the other half. When the process is complete, crimp the dough edges to seal, and bake according to directions.

Red Velvet-Berry Cobbler

A mashup of red velvet cake, berry cobbler, and trifle, this yummy dessert has everything you're craving in a sweet summer treat. Layer the cobbler with ice cream and berries in individual glasses.

1 Tbsp. cornstarch

1¼ cups granulated sugar, divided

6 cups assorted fresh berries (such as 2 cups each blackberries, raspberries, and blueberries.)

½ cup butter, softened

2 large eggs

2 Tbsp. red liquid food coloring

1 tsp. vanilla extract

1¼ cups all-purpose flour

1½ Tbsp. unsweetened cocoa

¼ tsp. table salt

½ cup buttermilk

1½ tsp. white vinegar

½ tsp. baking soda

Garnish: fresh mint sprigs

HANDS-ON: 20 MIN. ✦ **TOTAL:** 1 HR., 15 MIN.

1. Preheat oven to 350°.

2. Stir together cornstarch and ½ cup sugar. Toss berries with cornstarch mixture, and spoon into a lightly greased 11- x 7-inch baking dish.

3. Beat butter at medium speed with an electric mixer until fluffy; gradually add remaining ¾ cup sugar, beating well. Add eggs, 1 at a time, beating just until blended after each addition. Stir in red food coloring and vanilla until blended.

4. Combine flour, cocoa, and salt. Stir together buttermilk, vinegar, and baking soda in a 2-cup liquid measuring cup. (Mixture will bubble.) Add flour mixture to butter mixture alternately with buttermilk mixture, beginning and ending with flour mixture. Beat at low speed until blended after each addition. Spoon batter over berry mixture.

5. Bake at 350° for 45 to 50 minutes or until a wooden pick inserted in center of cake topping comes out clean. Cool on a wire rack 10 minutes. (Serves 6 to 8)

serve it on the side

Cream Cheese Ice Cream: Whisk together 3 cups half-and-half, 1¼ cups powdered sugar, and 2 egg yolks in a large heavy saucepan. Cook over medium heat, whisking constantly, 8 to 10 minutes or until mixture thickens slightly. Remove from heat, and whisk in 1 (8-oz.) package cream cheese and 2 tsp. vanilla bean paste or vanilla extract until cheese is melted. Cool completely (about 1 hour), stirring occasionally. Place plastic wrap directly on mixture (to prevent a film forming), and chill 8 to 24 hours. Pour mixture into freezer container of a 1½-qt. electric ice-cream maker, and freeze according to manufacturer's instructions. Transfer ice cream to an airtight container. Freeze 4 hours before serving. (Makes about 1 qt.)

Banana Bread Cobbler

Once you've made this simple streusel-topped cobbler, you'll never go back to traditional banana bread again. Drizzle your serving with heavy cream for even more indulgence and richness.

1 cup self-rising flour
1 cup granulated sugar
1 cup milk
½ cup butter, melted
4 medium-size ripe bananas,
    sliced
Streusel Topping

HANDS-ON: 15 MIN. ✦ **TOTAL:** 55 MIN.

1. Preheat oven to 375°.

2. Whisk together flour and next 2 ingredients just until blended; whisk in melted butter. Pour batter into a lightly greased 11- x 7-inch baking dish. Top with banana slices, and sprinkle with Streusel Topping.

3. Bake at 375° for 40 to 45 minutes or until golden brown and bubbly. (Serves 8)

Streusel Topping

HANDS-ON: 10 MIN. ✦ **TOTAL:** 10 MIN.

¾ cup firmly packed light brown sugar
½ cup self-rising flour
½ cup butter, softened

1 cup uncooked regular oats
½ cup chopped pecans

Stir together brown sugar and next 2 ingredients until crumbly. Stir in oats and pecans. (Makes 3½ cups)

Blackberry-Peach Cobbler with Praline-Pecan Streusel

We can't think of anything much better than a fresh summer peach cobbler topped with homemade vanilla ice cream. That is until we made this cobbler with blackberries and streusel topping.

STREUSEL

¾ cup firmly packed light brown sugar

½ cup butter, melted

⅛ tsp. table salt

1½ cups all-purpose flour

1 cup coarsely chopped pecans

FILLING

4 cups peeled and sliced fresh peaches (about 4 large)

½ cup granulated sugar

3 Tbsp. all-purpose flour

¼ tsp. ground nutmeg

2 cups fresh blackberries

HANDS-ON: 35 MIN. ✦ **TOTAL:** 1 HR., 10 MIN.

1. **Prepare Streusel:** Stir together first 3 ingredients in a large bowl; add flour and pecans, and stir until blended. Let stand 20 minutes or until mixture is firm enough to crumble into small pieces.

2. **Prepare Filling:** Preheat oven to 375°. Stir together peaches and next 3 ingredients in a large saucepan; bring to a boil over medium-high heat. Reduce heat to medium, and boil, stirring occasionally, 6 to 7 minutes or until juices have thickened. Remove from heat, and stir in blackberries. Spoon mixture into a lightly greased 9-inch square baking dish. Crumble streusel over hot peach mixture.

3. Bake at 375° for 30 to 35 minutes or until bubbly and golden brown. (Serves 8)

Bananas Foster Upside-Down Cake

The cast-iron skillet is essential to this cake—it helps create the golden crust that slips right out of the skillet and onto your plate.

½ cup chopped pecans

½ cup butter, softened and divided

1 cup firmly packed light brown sugar

2 Tbsp. rum

2 ripe bananas

¾ cup granulated sugar

2 large eggs

¾ cup milk

½ cup sour cream

1 tsp. vanilla extract

2 cups all-purpose baking mix

¼ tsp. ground cinnamon

HANDS-ON: 20 MIN. ✦ **TOTAL:** 1 HR., 18 MIN.

1. Preheat oven to 350°.

2. Bake pecans in a single layer 8 to 10 minutes or until toasted and fragrant, stirring once.

3. Melt ¼ cup butter in a lightly greased 10-inch cast-iron skillet over low heat. Remove from heat; stir in brown sugar and rum.

4. Cut bananas diagonally into ¼-inch-thick slices; arrange in concentric circles over brown sugar mixture. Sprinkle pecans over bananas.

5. Beat granulated sugar and remaining ¼ cup butter at medium speed with an electric mixer until blended. Add eggs, 1 at a time, beating just until blended after each addition. Add milk and next 2 ingredients; beat just until blended. Beat in baking mix and cinnamon until blended. (Batter will be slightly lumpy.) Pour batter over mixture in skillet, and spread to cover. Place skillet on an aluminum foil-lined jelly-roll pan.

6. Bake at 350° for 40 to 45 minutes or until a wooden pick inserted in center comes out clean. Cool in skillet on a wire rack 10 minutes. Run a knife around edge to loosen. Invert onto a serving plate, spooning any topping in skillet over cake. (Serves 8)

Peach Upside-Down Cake

This recipe calls for cake flour, which is very fine wheat flour ideal for pastries. Be sure to use cake flour and not all-purpose, as cake flour has much less protein and therefore creates less gluten, leaving you with a moist and tender cake.

Parchment paper

4 medium peaches (about 1½ lb.), unpeeled and cut into ⅓-inch-thick wedges

2 Tbsp. fresh lemon juice (about 1 large lemon)

1 cup cake flour

¾ tsp. baking powder

¼ tsp. baking soda

1¼ cups granulated sugar, divided

¾ cup unsalted butter, at room temperature and divided

½ cup firmly packed light brown sugar

1 vanilla bean

2 large eggs

½ cup sour cream

Sweetened whipped cream (optional)

HANDS-ON: 40 MIN. ✦ **TOTAL:** 40 MIN.

1. Preheat oven to 350°.

2. Line a baking sheet with parchment paper. In a bowl, toss peaches with lemon juice. In a separate bowl, sift together flour, baking powder, and baking soda.

3. Cook ½ cup granulated sugar in a 10-inch cast-iron skillet over medium heat, stirring occasionally with a wooden spoon, 10 minutes or until sugar melts and turns a deep amber color. Remove from heat. Immediately add ¼ cup butter, stirring vigorously. Spread caramelized sugar to coat bottom of skillet evenly, and sprinkle with brown sugar. Arrange peach wedges in concentric circles over sugar mixture.

4. Split vanilla bean lengthwise, and scrape out seeds into bowl of a heavy-duty electric stand mixer. Beat vanilla seeds and remaining ¾ cup granulated sugar and ½ cup butter at medium speed until smooth. Add eggs, 1 at a time, beating until blended after each addition. Add sour cream, beating until blended. Gradually add sifted flour mixture, beating at low speed just until blended and stopping to scrape bowl as needed. Spoon batter over peaches in skillet, and spread to cover. Place skillet on prepared baking sheet.

5. Bake at 350° for 40 to 45 minutes or until golden brown and a wooden pick inserted in center comes out clean. Cool in skillet on a wire rack 10 minutes. Run a knife around edge to loosen. Invert onto a serving plate, spooning any topping in skillet over cake. Top each serving with sweetened whipped cream, if desired. (Serves 8 to 12)

Pineapple Upside-Down Carrot Cake

This dessert creation combines the best of two beloved cakes—carrot cake and pineapple upside-down cake. The easy prep and sugary sweet flavor will make it a hit with you and your family.

¼ cup butter

⅔ cup firmly packed brown sugar

1 (20-oz.) can pineapple slices in juice, drained

7 maraschino cherries (without stems)

1 cup granulated sugar

½ cup vegetable oil

2 large eggs

1 cup all-purpose flour

1 tsp. baking powder

1 tsp. ground cinnamon

¾ tsp. baking soda

½ tsp. table salt

1½ cups grated carrots

½ cup finely chopped pecans

HANDS-ON: 20 MIN. ✦ **TOTAL:** 1 HR., 15 MIN.

1. Preheat oven to 350°.

2. Melt butter in a lightly greased 10-inch cast-iron skillet over low heat. Remove from heat. Sprinkle with brown sugar. Arrange 7 pineapple slices in a single layer over brown sugar, reserving remaining pineapple slices for another use. Place 1 cherry in center of each pineapple slice.

3. Beat granulated sugar, oil, and eggs at medium speed with an electric mixer until blended. Combine flour and next 4 ingredients; gradually add to sugar mixture, beating at low speed just until blended. Stir in carrots and pecans. Spoon batter over pineapple slices.

4. Bake at 350° for 45 to 50 minutes or until a wooden pick inserted in center comes out clean. Cool in skillet on a wire rack 10 minutes. Carefully run a knife around edge of cake to loosen. Invert cake onto a serving plate, spooning any topping in skillet over cake. (Serves 8)

Quick Apple Dumpling Bundles

Guests will love getting their own little apple goodies topped with luscious, warm caramel.

½ cup chopped pecans

½ (14.1-oz.) package refrigerated
   piecrusts

1 (12-oz.) package frozen spiced
   apples, thawed

1 large egg white, lightly beaten

Granulated sugar

1 (12-oz.) jar caramel topping,
   warmed

HANDS-ON: 20 MIN. ✦ **TOTAL:** 40 MIN.

1. Preheat oven to 350°. Bake pecans in a single layer in a shallow pan 5 to 6 minutes or until toasted and fragrant. Remove from oven; increase oven temperature to 425°.

2. Unroll piecrust on a lightly floured surface. Cut piecrust into fourths. Divide apples among each fourth, placing in center. Pull corners together over apples, pinching edges to seal. Place on a lightly greased aluminum foil-lined baking sheet; brush with egg white, and sprinkle with sugar.

3. Bake at 425° for 20 minutes or until golden. Serve apple bundles with warm caramel topping. Sprinkle with pecans. (Serves 4)

NOTE: *We tested with Stouffer's Harvest Apples and Smucker's Caramel Flavored Topping.*

Apple Brown Betty

This classic dessert is almost as American as apple pie. It's layered and garnished with a sweetened breadcrumb topping instead of piecrust.

4 cups soft, fresh breadcrumbs

⅓ cup butter, melted

1 cup firmly packed brown sugar

1 Tbsp. ground cinnamon

4 large Granny Smith apples, peeled and cut into ¼-inch-thick slices

1 cup apple cider

HANDS-ON: 15 MIN. ✦ **TOTAL:** 1 HR.

1. Preheat oven to 350°.

2. Stir together breadcrumbs and butter. Stir together brown sugar and cinnamon. Place half of apple slices in a lightly greased 8-inch square baking dish; sprinkle apples with half of brown sugar mixture and half of breadcrumb mixture. Repeat procedure with remaining apples, brown sugar mixture, and breadcrumb mixture. Pour apple cider over top.

3. Bake at 350° for 45 to 55 minutes or until browned. (Serves 6)

serve it on the side

Vanilla Bean Ice Cream: Whisk together ¾ cup sugar, 2 Tbsp. cornstarch, and ⅛ tsp. table salt in a large heavy saucepan. Gradually whisk in 2 cups milk and 1 cup heavy whipping cream. Cook over medium heat, stirring constantly, 10 to 12 minutes, or until mixture thickens and coats a spoon. (Do not boil.) Remove from heat. Whisk 1 large egg yolk until slightly thickened. Gradually whisk about 1 cup hot cream mixture into yolk. Add yolk mixture to remaining cream mixture, whisking constantly. Whisk in 1½ tsp. vanilla bean paste. Cool 1 hour, stirring occasionally. Place plastic wrap directly on cream mixture, and chill 8 to 24 hours. Pour mixture into freezer container of 1½-qt. electric ice-cream maker, and freeze according to manufacturer's instructions. (Instructions and times will vary.) (Makes about 1 qt.)

Peach-Rhubarb Crisp

Rhubarb, which is known for its tart flavor, adds a bright red color to this summer fruit crisp. Replace the peaches with one 10-ounce bag frozen strawberries for a traditional strawberry and rhubarb crisp.

1 (20-oz.) bag frozen peaches, thawed

2 (16-oz.) packages frozen sliced rhubarb, thawed

1½ cups granulated sugar

3 Tbsp. fresh lemon juice

1¼ cups all-purpose flour, divided

Vegetable cooking spray

⅓ cup uncooked quick-cooking oats

⅓ cup firmly packed brown sugar

⅓ cup cold butter, cut into small pieces

HANDS-ON: 15 MIN. ✦ **TOTAL:** 1 HR., 5 MIN.

1. Preheat oven to 375°. Combine first 4 ingredients in a medium bowl; add ¼ cup flour, stirring well. Pour mixture into a 13- x 9-inch baking dish coated with cooking spray.

2. Combine oats, brown sugar, and remaining 1 cup flour in a small bowl; cut in cold butter with a fork or pastry blender until mixture resembles coarse crumbs. Sprinkle mixture evenly over filling.

3. Bake at 375° for 45 to 50 minutes or until bubbly. (Serves 10)

— *serve it on the side* —

Spiked Strawberry Milk: Process 1 qt. fresh, hulled strawberries and 3 to 4 Tbsp. sugar in a blender until smooth, stopping to scrape down sides as needed. Press mixture through a wire-mesh strainer into a medium bowl, using back of a spoon to squeeze out juice; discard pulp. Stir in 1 tsp. vanilla extract and pinch of salt. Stir strawberry mixture into 3 to 4 cups cold milk. Chill 1 hour before serving. Refrigerate up to 3 days. Stir in ¼ cup strawberry liqueur (such as De Kuyper Wild Strawberry) just before serving. (Makes about 6 cups)

Skillet Apple Pie

The Granny Smith apples in this skillet apple pie are typically known as the go-to apple for baking because they hold up to heat, and they have a wonderful balance of sweet and tart flavors.

2 lb. Granny Smith apples

2 lb. Braeburn apples

1 tsp. ground cinnamon

¾ cup granulated sugar

½ cup butter

1 cup firmly packed light brown sugar

1 (14.1-oz.) package refrigerated piecrusts

1 large egg white

2 Tbsp. granulated sugar

HANDS-ON: 20 MIN. ✦ **TOTAL:** 1 HR., 50 MIN.

1. Preheat oven to 350°.

2. Peel apples, and cut into ½-inch-thick wedges. Toss apples with cinnamon and ¾ cup granulated sugar.

3. Melt butter in a 10-inch cast-iron skillet over medium heat; add brown sugar, and cook, stirring constantly, 1 to 2 minutes or until sugar dissolves. Remove from heat, and place 1 piecrust in skillet over brown sugar mixture. Spoon apple mixture over piecrust, and top with remaining piecrust. Whisk egg white until foamy. Brush top of piecrust with egg white; sprinkle with 2 Tbsp. granulated sugar. Cut 4 or 5 slits in top for steam to escape.

4. Bake at 350° for 1 hour to 1 hour and 10 minutes or until golden brown and bubbly, shielding with aluminum foil during last 10 minutes to prevent excessive browning, if necessary. Cool on a wire rack 30 minutes before serving. (Serves 8 to 10)

serve it on the side

Vanilla-Cinnamon Ice Cream: Stir together 1 qt. store-bought vanilla ice cream, softened; ¼ cup milk; 2 Tbsp. firmly packed brown sugar; and ¼ tsp. ground cinnamon. Freeze 1 hour. (Makes 7½ cups)

Caramel Apple Blondie Pie

Tender cake and caramelized apples, bourbon, pecans, and sweet caramel sauce all come together to make this a favorite fall dessert. And the secret to achieving the perfect flaky crust? Baking in a cast-iron skillet on a lower oven rack. Who knew?

6 large Granny Smith apples
  (about 3 lb.)
2 Tbsp. all-purpose flour
2 cups firmly packed light
  brown sugar, divided
1 cup butter, divided
1½ cups all-purpose flour
1½ tsp. baking powder
½ tsp. table salt
3 large eggs, lightly beaten
3 Tbsp. bourbon
¾ cup coarsely chopped toasted
  pecans
½ (14.1-oz.) package refrigerated
  piecrusts
Apple Cider Caramel Sauce

HANDS-ON: 40 MIN. ✦ **TOTAL:** 2 HR., 57 MIN., INCLUDING SAUCE

1. Peel apples, and cut into ¼-inch-thick wedges. Toss with 2 Tbsp. flour and ½ cup brown sugar in a large bowl. Melt ¼ cup butter in a large skillet over medium-high heat; add apple mixture, and sauté 15 minutes or until apples are tender and liquid is thickened. Remove from heat; cool completely (about 30 minutes).

2. Meanwhile, preheat oven to 350°. Melt remaining ¾ cup butter. Stir together 1½ cups flour and next 2 ingredients in a large bowl. Add eggs, bourbon, ¾ cup melted butter, and remaining 1½ cups brown sugar, stirring until blended. Stir in pecans.

3. Fit piecrust into a 10-inch cast-iron skillet, gently pressing piecrust all the way up the sides of skillet. Spoon ⅔ of apple mixture over bottom of piecrust, spreading and gently pressing apple slices into an even layer using the back of a spoon. Spoon batter over apple mixture; top with remaining apple mixture.

4. Place pie on lower oven rack, and bake at 350° for 1 hour and 10 minutes to 1 hour and 20 minutes or until a wooden pick inserted in center comes out with a few moist crumbs. Remove from oven; cool completely on a wire rack.

5. Drizzle with ⅓ cup Apple Cider Caramel Sauce. Serve with remaining sauce. (Serves 8 to 10)

Apple Cider Caramel Sauce

HANDS-ON: 12 MIN. ✦ **TOTAL:** 12 MIN.

1 cup apple cider
1 cup firmly packed light brown sugar

½ cup butter
¼ cup whipping cream

1. Cook cider in a 3-qt. saucepan over medium heat, stirring often, 10 minutes or until reduced to ¼ cup.

2. Stir in remaining ingredients. Bring to a boil over medium-high heat, stirring constantly; boil, stirring constantly, 2 minutes. Remove from heat, and cool completely. Refrigerate up to 1 week. (Makes about 1¼ cups)

Caramel-Pecan-Pumpkin Bread Puddings

Fall flavors come together in this rich pumpkin bread pudding. Whip it together in minutes the day before you plan to serve it, and all you have to do the day of is pop it in the oven, make the creamy caramel sauce, and enjoy.

BREAD PUDDINGS

4 large eggs

2 (15-oz.) cans pumpkin

1½ cups milk

1 cup half-and-half

1 cup granulated sugar

1 tsp. ground cinnamon

½ tsp. table salt

½ tsp. ground nutmeg

½ tsp. vanilla extract

1 (12-oz.) French bread loaf,
cut into 1-inch pieces
(about 10 cups)

CARAMEL-PECAN SAUCE

1 cup pecans, chopped

1 cup firmly packed light brown
sugar

½ cup butter

1 Tbsp. light corn syrup

1 tsp. vanilla extract

HANDS-ON: 27 MIN. ✦ **TOTAL:** 9 HR., 22 MIN., INCLUDING CHILL TIME

1. **Prepare Bread Puddings:** Whisk together eggs and next 8 ingredients in a large bowl until well blended. Add bread, stirring to thoroughly coat. Cover with plastic wrap, and chill 8 to 24 hours.

2. Preheat oven to 350°.

3. Spoon bread mixture into 11 (6-oz.) lightly greased ramekins. (Ramekins will be completely full, and mixture will mound slightly.) Place on an aluminum foil-lined jelly-roll pan.

4. Bake at 350° for 50 minutes, shielding with foil after 30 minutes.

5. During last 15 minutes of baking, prepare **Caramel-Pecan Sauce:** Heat pecans in a medium skillet over medium-low heat, stirring often, 3 to 5 minutes or until lightly toasted and fragrant.

6. Cook brown sugar, butter, and corn syrup in a small saucepan over medium heat, stirring occasionally, 3 to 4 minutes or until sugar is dissolved. Remove from heat; stir in vanilla and pecans.

7. Remove bread puddings from oven; drizzle with Caramel-Pecan Sauce. Bake 5 more minutes or until sauce is thoroughly heated and begins to bubble. (Serves 11)

Cornbread Pudding

Use your leftover cornbread to make this dessert treat. A little whiskey goes a long way in the caramel topping.

Perfect Cornbread, cooled
½ cup butter
2 cups milk
1 cup granulated sugar
1 Tbsp. vanilla extract
1½ tsp. kosher salt
5 large eggs
Whiskey Caramel Sauce

HANDS-ON: 15 MIN.   ✦   **TOTAL:** 3 HR., INCLUDING CORNBREAD AND SAUCE

1. Preheat oven to 350°. Lightly grease a 3-qt. baking dish. Cube cornbread into 2-inch pieces (about 10 cups), and place in prepared dish. Cook butter in a 2-qt. saucepan over medium heat, stirring constantly, until it begins to turn golden brown. Remove from heat, and whisk in milk and next 3 ingredients until sugar melts. Whisk in eggs; pour mixture over cornbread. Let stand 10 minutes.

2. Bake, covered, for 30 minutes. Uncover and bake 30 more minutes or until light brown and set. Let stand 10 minutes. Serve with Whiskey Caramel Sauce. (Serves 8 to 10)

Perfect Cornbread

HANDS-ON: 20 MIN.   ✦   **TOTAL:** 55 MIN.

1 cup plain yellow cornmeal
1 cup all-purpose flour
1 Tbsp. baking powder
1 tsp. kosher salt
¼ tsp. baking soda
2 cups buttermilk
2 large eggs
½ cup butter

Preheat oven to 425°. Whisk together first 5 ingredients in a bowl. Whisk together buttermilk and eggs; stir into cornmeal mixture just until combined. Heat a 10-inch cast-iron skillet over medium-high heat until it begins to smoke. Add butter, and stir until melted. Stir melted butter into cornbread batter. Pour batter into hot skillet. Bake for 25 to 30 minutes or until golden and pulls away from sides. Cool on wire rack. (Serves 8 to 10)

Whiskey Caramel Sauce

HANDS-ON: 30 MIN.   ✦   **TOTAL:** 30 MIN.

1½ cups granulated sugar, divided
½ cup heavy cream
½ cup butter, cubed
¼ cup whiskey
¼ tsp. kosher salt
¼ tsp. ground nutmeg
1 large egg

Stir together 1 cup sugar and ¼ cup water in a saucepan. Cook over medium-high heat, stirring constantly, 3 minutes or until sugar melts. Cook, without stirring, 10 minutes or until medium amber in color. Remove from heat, and stir in next 5 ingredients. Whisk together egg and remaining ½ cup sugar in a heatproof medium bowl; slowly whisk caramel sauce into egg mixture. Return mixture to saucepan, and cook over medium heat, stirring constantly, 2 minutes or until thickened. (Makes 2 cups)

Café Brûlot Bread Pudding

Chicory coffee, cinnamon, and cloves spice up this decadent dessert. It's named for an after-dinner drink served in legendary New Orleans restaurants like Galatoire's and Arnaud's.

3 large eggs

2 cups milk

1 cup granulated sugar

1 cup strong brewed chicory coffee

¼ cup butter, melted

1 Tbsp. firmly packed orange zest

¼ cup fresh orange juice

¾ tsp. ground cinnamon

¼ tsp. table salt

⅛ tsp. ground cloves

1 (8-oz.) French bread loaf, cut into 1-inch cubes

Café Brûlot Sauce

HANDS-ON: 20 MIN. ✦ **TOTAL:** 1 HR., 30 MIN., INCLUDING SAUCE

1. Preheat oven to 325°.

2. Whisk together first 10 ingredients in a large bowl. Add bread cubes; cover and chill 10 minutes. Spoon bread mixture into a lightly greased 11- x 7-inch baking dish.

3. Bake at 325° for 1 hour or until set. Serve immediately with Café Brûlot Sauce. (Serves 10)

Café Brûlot Sauce

HANDS-ON: 10 MIN. ✦ **TOTAL:** 10 MIN.

½ cup butter

½ cup granulated sugar

¼ cup heavy cream

1 Tbsp. strong brewed chicory coffee

1 Tbsp. brandy

1 tsp. firmly packed orange zest

Cook butter and sugar in heavy saucepan over low heat, stirring constantly, 3 minutes or until smooth. Stir in heavy cream and chicory coffee. Cook, stirring constantly, 5 minutes or until thickened. Remove from heat; stir in brandy and orange zest. (Makes 1 cup)

Mexican Chocolate Pudding Cake

Red pepper, chipotle chile pepper, and cinnamon combine to give this decadent chocolate pudding cake a subtle touch of heat. The molten center and crispy almonds create the ultimate texture combination—you'll have a hard time putting your spoon down.

1½ cups semisweet chocolate morsels
½ cup butter
¾ cup granulated sugar
4 large eggs
1 cup all-purpose flour
½ tsp. ground cinnamon
¼ tsp. baking powder
¼ tsp. ground red pepper
¼ tsp. ground chipotle chile pepper
½ tsp. kosher salt, divided
½ cup sliced almonds
2 tsp. olive oil
1 tsp. light brown sugar

HANDS-ON: 30 MIN.   ✦   **TOTAL:** 1 HR., 10 MIN.

1. Preheat oven to 350°. Microwave chocolate and butter in a large microwave-safe bowl at HIGH 1 to 1½ minutes or until melted, stirring at 30-second intervals. Whisk in granulated sugar. Add eggs, 1 at a time, whisking just until blended after each addition. Whisk in flour, next 4 ingredients, and ¼ tsp. salt.

2. Pour batter into a greased (with butter) 2-qt. baking dish. Stir together sliced almonds, next 2 ingredients, and remaining ¼ tsp. salt. Sprinkle almond mixture over cake batter. Bake at 350° for 30 minutes. (Center will be soft.) Cool on a wire rack 5 minutes. Serve warm. (Serves 6)

Mocha Java Cakes

These chocolate soufflés are as sinful as you'd think—but much easier to prepare than you'd expect.

1 cup butter, plus 1 Tbsp. butter, divided
8 oz. bittersweet chocolate morsels
4 large egg yolks
4 large eggs
2 cups powdered sugar
¾ cup all-purpose flour
1 tsp. instant espresso or instant coffee granules
Pinch of table salt
Garnish: powdered sugar

HANDS-ON: 15 MIN. ✦ **TOTAL:** 31 MIN.

1. Preheat oven to 425°.

2. Grease 6 (6-oz.) ramekins or individual soufflé dishes with 1 Tbsp. butter.

3. Microwave remaining 1 cup butter and chocolate morsels in a large microwave-safe bowl at HIGH 1½ to 2 minutes or until melted and smooth, stirring at 30-second intervals.

4. Beat egg yolks and eggs at medium speed with an electric mixer 1 minute. Gradually add chocolate mixture, beating at low speed until well blended.

5. Sift together sugar and next 3 ingredients. Gradually whisk sugar mixture into chocolate mixture until well blended. Divide batter among prepared ramekins. Place ramekins in a 15- x 10-inch jelly-roll pan.

6. Bake at 425° for 16 minutes or until a thermometer inserted into cakes registers 165°. Remove from oven, and let stand 10 minutes. Run a knife around outer edge of each cake to loosen. Carefully invert cakes onto dessert plates. (Serves 6)

NOTE: *We tested with Ghirardelli 60% Cacao Bittersweet Chocolate Chips.*

mix it up

Minty-Mocha Java Cakes: Prepare recipe as directed through Step 5. Chop 12 thin crème de menthe chocolate mints. Sprinkle center of batter in ramekins with chopped mints. Press mints into batter gently just until submerged. Proceed with recipe as directed in Step 6.

Note: *We tested with Andes Crème de Menthe Thins.*

Orange-Mocha Java Cakes: Prepare recipe as directed through Step 4. Sift together sugar and next 3 ingredients. Gradually whisk sugar mixture into chocolate mixture until well blended. Whisk in ¼ cup orange liqueur and 1 tsp. orange zest. Divide batter among prepared ramekins. Place ramekins in a 15- x 10-inch jelly-roll pan. Proceed with recipe as directed in Step 6, baking cakes 14 to 16 minutes or until a thermometer inserted into cakes registers 165°.

Note: *We tested with Grand Marnier.*

Gingerbread Soufflés

Even gingerbread men have to admit these soufflés are superior. Pop them in the oven just before dinner and they'll be done by the time you're finished eating.

1 cup milk
½ cup sugar
¼ cup all-purpose flour
¼ tsp. table salt
⅓ cup molasses
2 Tbsp. butter, softened
2 tsp. pumpkin pie spice
1 tsp. ground ginger
2 tsp. vanilla extract
6 large eggs, separated
⅛ tsp. cream of tartar
Garnishes: sweetened whipped cream, crushed gingersnaps

HANDS-ON: 20 MIN.　✦　**TOTAL:** 1 HR., 30 MIN.

1. Preheat oven to 350°.

2. Whisk together first 4 ingredients in a medium saucepan until smooth. Bring to a boil over medium heat, whisking constantly. Transfer mixture to a large bowl, and whisk in molasses and next 4 ingredients. Cool 15 minutes. Whisk in egg yolks.

3. Grease 10 (7-oz.) ramekins; sprinkle with sugar to coat, and shake out excess.

4. Beat egg whites and cream of tartar at high speed with an electric mixer until stiff peaks form. Fold one-third of egg white mixture into milk mixture until well blended. Repeat twice with remaining egg white mixture. Spoon batter into prepared ramekins, leaving ¾-inch space at top of each.

5. Bake at 350° for 25 minutes or until puffy and set. Serve immediately. (Serves 10)

NOTE: *You can also bake this in a 2½-qt. soufflé dish. Bake at 350° for 55 to 60 minutes or until puffy and set.*

White Chocolate-Cranberry Crème Brûlée

Try this take on traditional crème brûlée—the addition of cranberry into the ingredients makes this an ideal dessert during the holidays.

2 cups whipping cream

1 (4-oz.) sweet white chocolate baking bar

1 tsp. vanilla extract

5 egg yolks

½ cup sugar, divided

½ (14-oz.) can whole-berry cranberry sauce

Ice cubes

Garnish: fresh sugared cranberries

HANDS-ON: 30 MIN. ✦ **TOTAL:** 9 HR., 20 MIN., INCLUDING CHILL TIME

1. Preheat oven to 300°.

2. Combine ½ cup cream and chocolate in a heavy saucepan; cook over low heat, stirring constantly, 2 to 3 minutes or until chocolate melts. Remove from heat. Stir in vanilla and remaining 1½ cups cream.

3. Whisk together egg yolks and ¼ cup sugar until sugar dissolves and mixture is thick and pale yellow. Add cream mixture, whisking until well blended. Pour mixture through a fine wire-mesh strainer into a large bowl.

4. Spoon 1½ Tbsp. cranberry sauce into each of 6 (4-oz.) ramekins. Pour cream mixture into ramekins; place ramekins in a large roasting pan. Add water to pan to depth of ½ inch.

5. Bake at 300° for 45 to 55 minutes or until edges are set. Cool custards in pan on a wire rack 25 minutes. Remove ramekins from water; cover and chill 8 hours.

6. Preheat broiler with oven rack 5 inches from heat. Sprinkle remaining sugar over ramekins. Fill a large roasting pan or 15- x 10-inch jelly-roll pan with ice; arrange ramekins in pan.

7. Broil 3 to 5 minutes or until sugar is melted and caramelized. Let stand 5 minutes. (Serves 6)

mix it up

White Chocolate-Banana Crème Brûlée: Prepare recipe as directed through Step 3. Slice 2 bananas into ¼-inch-thick slices; toss bananas with ⅓ cup sugar. Melt 2 Tbsp. butter in a large nonstick skillet over medium-high heat. Add bananas, and cook 1 to 2 minutes on each side or until lightly browned. Line bottoms of 6 (4-oz.) ramekins evenly with banana slices. Pour cream mixture evenly into ramekins; place ramekins in a large roasting pan. Add water to pan to depth of ½ inch. Proceed with recipe as directed in Step 5. (Serves 6)

Sweet Tea Tiramisù

How does the South do Italian tiramisù? By replacing espresso with sweet tea, of course!

2 family-size tea bags

1½ cups sugar, divided

2 (8-oz.) containers mascarpone cheese

1 Tbsp. vanilla bean paste or vanilla extract

2 cups whipping cream

2 (3-oz.) packages ladyfingers

1 to 2 tsp. unsweetened cocoa

HANDS-ON: 20 MIN. ✦ **TOTAL:** 13 HR., 30 MIN., INCLUDING CHILL TIME

1. Bring 4 cups water to a boil in a 3-qt. heavy saucepan; add tea bags. Remove from heat; cover and steep 10 minutes.

2. Discard tea bags. Add 1 cup sugar, stirring until dissolved. Bring tea mixture to a boil over medium-high heat, and cook, stirring occasionally, 20 to 22 minutes or until mixture is reduced to 1 cup. Remove mixture from heat, and cool to room temperature (about 30 minutes).

3. Stir together mascarpone cheese, vanilla bean paste, and remaining ½ cup sugar.

4. Beat whipping cream at medium speed with an electric mixer until soft peaks form; fold into cheese mixture.

5. Separate ladyfingers in half. Arrange 24 ladyfinger halves, flat sides up, in the bottom of an 11- x 7-inch baking dish. Drizzle with half of tea mixture. Top with half of cheese mixture. Repeat layers once. Cover and chill 12 hours. Sift cocoa over top just before serving. (Serves 10 to 12)

dress it up

Add fresh fruit and chocolate to round out the rich flavors.
Toss sliced strawberries and pitted fresh cherries with a little sugar and almond liqueur; add shaved chocolate. Dollop atop Sweet Tea Tiramisù.

METRIC EQUIVALENTS

The recipes that appear in this cookbook use the standard U.S. method for measuring liquid and dry or solid ingredients (teaspoons, tablespoons, and cups). The information on this chart is provided to help cooks outside the United States successfully use these recipes. All equivalents are approximate.

METRIC EQUIVALENTS FOR DIFFERENT TYPES OF INGREDIENTS

A standard cup measure of a dry or solid ingredient will vary in weight depending on the type of ingredient. A standard cup of liquid is the same volume for any type of liquid. Use the following chart when converting standard cup measures to grams (weight) or milliliters (volume).

Standard Cup	Fine Powder (ex. flour)	Grain (ex. rice)	Granular (ex. sugar)	Liquid Solids (ex. butter)	Liquid (ex. milk)
1	140 g	150 g	190 g	200 g	240 ml
¾	105 g	113 g	143 g	150 g	180 ml
⅔	93 g	100 g	125 g	133 g	160 ml
½	70 g	75 g	95 g	100 g	120 ml
⅓	47 g	50 g	63 g	67 g	80 ml
¼	35 g	38 g	48 g	50 g	60 ml
⅛	18 g	19 g	24 g	25 g	30 ml

USEFUL EQUIVALENTS FOR DRY INGREDIENTS BY WEIGHT

(To convert ounces to grams, multiply the number of ounces by 30.)

1 oz	=	1/16 lb	=	30 g
4 oz	=	¼ lb	=	120 g
8 oz	=	½ lb	=	240 g
12 oz	=	¾ lb	=	360 g
16 oz	=	1 lb	=	480 g

USEFUL EQUIVALENTS FOR LENGTH

(To convert inches to centimeters, multiply the number of inches by 2.5.)

1 in				=	2.5 cm		
6 in	=	½ ft		=	15 cm		
12 in	=	1 ft		=	30 cm		
36 in	=	3 ft	=	1 yd	=	90 cm	
40 in				=	100 cm	=	1 m

USEFUL EQUIVALENTS FOR LIQUID INGREDIENTS BY VOLUME

¼ tsp						=	1 ml	
½ tsp						=	2 ml	
1 tsp						=	5 ml	
3 tsp	=	1 Tbsp		=	½ fl oz	=	15 ml	
		2 Tbsp	=	⅛ cup	=	1 fl oz	=	30 ml	
		4 Tbsp	=	¼ cup	=	2 fl oz	=	60 ml	
		5⅓ Tbsp	=	⅓ cup	=	3 fl oz	=	80 ml	
		8 Tbsp	=	½ cup	=	4 fl oz	=	120 ml	
		10⅔ Tbsp	=	⅔ cup	=	5 fl oz	=	160 ml	
		12 Tbsp	=	¾ cup	=	6 fl oz	=	180 ml	
		16 Tbsp	=	1 cup	=	8 fl oz	=	240 ml	
		1 pt	=	2 cups	=	16 fl oz	=	480 ml	
		1 qt	=	4 cups	=	32 fl oz	=	960 ml	
						33 fl oz	=	1000 ml	= 1 l

USEFUL EQUIVALENTS FOR COOKING/OVEN TEMPERATURES

	Fahrenheit	Celsius	Gas Mark
Freeze water	32° F	0° C	
Room temperature	68° F	20° C	
Boil water	212° F	100° C	
Bake	325° F	160° C	3
	350° F	180° C	4
	375° F	190° C	5
	400° F	200° C	6
	425° F	220° C	7
	450° F	230° C	8
Broil			Grill

INDEX